BRAIN POWER

Working out the Human Mind

PROFESSOR SUSAN GREENFIELD

CONTRIBUTORS

Gregory Bacon
Clive Coen
Henry Marsh
Kim Plunkett
Nicholas Rawlins
John Stein

SHAFTESBURY, DORSET • BOSTON, MASSACHUSETTS • MELBOURNE, VICTORIA

First published in Great Britain in 1999 by

ELEMENT BOOKS LIMITED

Shaftesbury, Dorset SP7 8BP

Copyright © THE IVY PRESS LIMITED 1999

A CIP catalogue record for this book is
available from the British Library

Library of Congress CIP data is available

ISBN 1-86204-745-6

This book was conceived, designed,
and produced by

THE IVY PRESS LIMITED

The Old Candlemakers, West Street

Lewes, East Sussex, BN7 2NZ

Creative Director: PETER BRIDGEWATER

Art Director: ANDREW MILNE

Designer: JANE LANAWAY

Editorial Director: DENNY HEMMING

Editor: PETER LEEK

Photography: GUY RYECART

3D Models: MARK JAMIESON

Illustrations: IVAN HISSEY, CATHERINE MCINTYRE,

TONY SIMPSON, NICK PERRY

Picture Research: VANESSA FLETCHER, TRUDI VALTER

Printed and bound in China

Contents

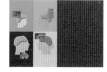

INTRODUCTION TO THE BRAIN

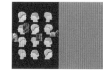

1 IN THE GENES

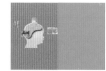

2 THE GROWING BRAIN

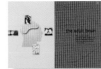

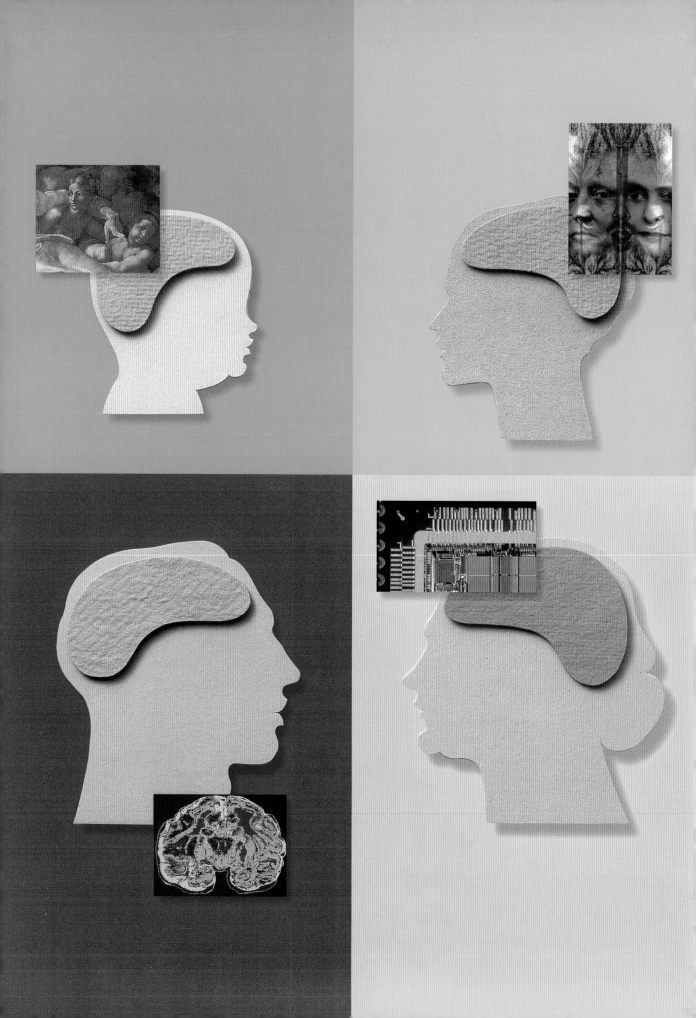

The human mind

We have recently left a decade behind us – the "Decade of the Brain" – a time officially celebrated for progress in brain research. But although the 1990s are over, the curtain is far from coming down on neuroscientists' endeavors.

Discoveries made during the previous ten years are not merely finishing touches to an accepted body of knowledge of how the brain works. Instead, recent research on the brain – much of which you are about to read here – is challenging many previous ideas and providing the basis for an exciting new era of discovery. And never before has such knowledge been needed. As we set out on a new century when we will be living longer, where we will have more leisure time, and where the organs below the neck will be transplanted with increasing ease, so attention becomes increasingly concentrated on the part of the body that gives us our identity – that special, private place, the human mind.

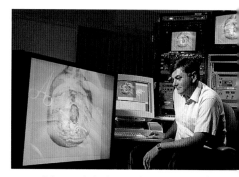

ABOVE Advances in brain scanning techniques and equipment have given us a much clearer picture of how the brain works, but new discoveries have also led to fresh questions.

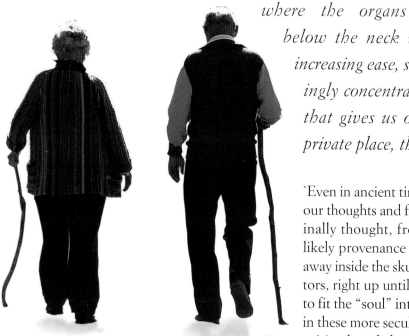

ABOVE As people live longer, it is becoming increasingly important to establish how we can best nurture and preserve our mental capacities into old age.

`Even in ancient times it was eventually realized that our thoughts and feelings emanated not, as was originally thought, from the lungs, but from the less likely provenance of the sludgy gray matter locked away inside the skull. Yet the problem for our ancestors, right up until the nineteenth century, was how to fit the "soul" into the equation – an equation that in these more secular times is not so mandatory. The spiritual, and above all immortal, soul was thought to be an entity that nonetheless had some tenuous relationship with the very obviously perishable physical brain. This distinction, propounded most

ABOVE The French philosopher René Descartes proposed that the spiritual and the material were separate realms, such that the soul or mind and the physical brain had no connection.

famously in the seventeenth century by the philosopher René Descartes, was to establish a certain way of thinking about the brain. On one hand, there was the wrinkled organ itself, as much a part of the physical body as the heart and the lungs; on the other were the completely intangible "mental" phenomena of thoughts and feelings that in some way could be separated from the mechanical workings of the body.

Some people – mainly philosophers – still agonize over how such duality might ever be realized (the "brain-mind problem"), but nowadays most scientists work from the stance that everything we think and feel, however improbable and untraceable it seems, must have some kind of physical basis rooted in the brain itself. The century that has just closed witnessed meticulous experiments and clinical observations proving, over and over again, that what happens in the physical brain is inextricably related to how we feel, think, and behave.

An explosion of interest

A photograph taken in Pavia in 1900 shows some hundred delegates at one of the earliest conferences on the study of nerve cells. By 1998, in striking contrast, the most recent meeting of the American Society for Neuroscience boasted 30,000 attendants. The brain presents the ultimate challenge. Whereas the heart can be likened readily to a pump and the lungs to bellows, the brain itself has no intrinsic moving parts. It offers no obvious clues to what is happening within, or to how those inner processes are actually translated into subjective feelings and private thoughts – and yet brain research is now allowing us to have a realistic chance of tackling these questions.

For example, we now have a clear idea as to how one brain cell – a neuron – communicates with the next cell along. In the first half of the twentieth century, controversy raged over whether this communication was an electrical phenomenon, or whether neurons were in fact separated by small gaps that could not be breached by electricity alone, but required a chemical intermediary – a "transmitter." Although there are instances where brain cells are fused together and propagate waves of electricity across each other, it is now established that transmission across a gap – "a synapse" – is the most common mechanism.

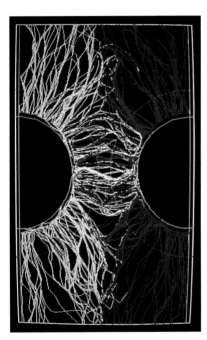

ABOVE Brain cells photographed through an electron microscope, showing the cell nuclei and dendrites.

ABOVE The size and complexity of the human brain is what sets us apart from all other animals, allowing us to survive in many different environments, to develop language, and to create works of art like Michelangelo's Sistine Chapel ceiling.

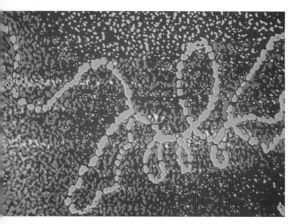

ABOVE A strand of human DNA, seen through an electron microscope. DNA is the basic element of most living organisms, including human beings.

Our flexible brains

At the most basic level, everything you are can be reduced to a simple alternating chain of events: an electrical blip generated in one cell causes a chemical to be released onto the next cell, causing a chemical to be released onto the next cell along, which in turn causes another electrical blip. This process of "synaptic transmission" inspired scientists in the 1960s and 1970s to think of the brain as a computer; at that time, of course, computers were themselves relatively unfamiliar, rare, and rather forbidding systems. But as more was discovered about the brain, the simple computer analogy began to become less and less popular. If all the operations of the brain could be reduced to binary on/off states, then why have such a treasure trove of different transmitters, ranging from large molecules folding in on themselves to simple gases? Perhaps, after all, in addition to simple one-time events, much more subtle and less familiar processes occur in the brain that require various types of chemical messenger.

We now know that many brain processes cannot simply be described by reference to switches that are either "on" or "off." Instead, the brain is in a constant state of change.

If you think about it, it is fairly obvious that the brain must undergo some kind of transformation every moment of your life – otherwise you wouldn't have a different consciousness from one moment to the next. But in addition to changing every second, the brain also needs to be able to adapt on a more long-term basis. This flexible quality is referred to by neuroscientists as "plasticity."

This plasticity enables the brain to adapt, to learn from the environment and from experience, even in some circumstances to compensate for damage or injury. This is why human beings, the species with the most adaptable brains, occupy the widest range of ecological niches on the planet. Indeed, it is a remarkable thought that our brains have not changed for the last 30,000 years, since the time when our ancestors first staggered out on two legs into the savanna. For reasons that are still not fully understood, our brains had the capacity to cater for the unique skill of language, and at the same time to permit any number of related talents, such as complex tool use, the practice of religion, and art – all the activities that make humans unique. And yet to look at, our brains do not appear very different from the brains of our nearest relatives, the chimpanzees, whose DNA is only one percent different from our own.

Size matters

What is it then that distinguishes our brains from those of our fellow primates? The biggest clue lies not in some new feature bolted exclusively onto the human brain – some new quality – but rather in quantity. In particular, at the front of the brain the outer coating of brain cells (the cortex) has twice the surface area we might expect for a primate of our body weight. Moreover, although we are born with brains that are more or less the same size as those of chimps, our human brains, unlike those of our simian cousins, proceed to undergo a startling expansion after birth. This expansion of our brain seems to match up with our very special human qualities.

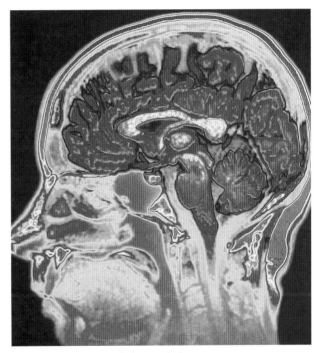

ABOVE Brain scans are beginning to unlock some of the brain's mysteries, allowing researchers to see the patterns of neurological activity that relate to particular processes.

However, it is not the case that we suddenly started to produce more brain cells. We are – and it is a sobering thought – born with almost all the brain cells we are ever going to have. Rather, the connections between the cells grow at an astonishing rate, becoming ever longer and denser after birth, so that complex networks of neurons gradually form. This postnatal growth of brain-cell connections is especially marked in humans and allows for a unique configuration of each brain. And this would even be the case with human clones. So, no matter whether you were born 30,000 years ago or at the same time as Christopher Columbus or a short time ago, in the Amazon jungle or in a densely populated city, the brain always starts off the same, but then adapts to suit your particular lifestyle, your unique life.

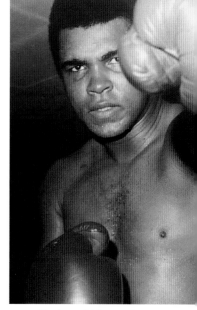

ABOVE The boxer Muhammad Ali is a famous sufferer from Parkinson's disease, probably as a result of his high-risk sporting career.

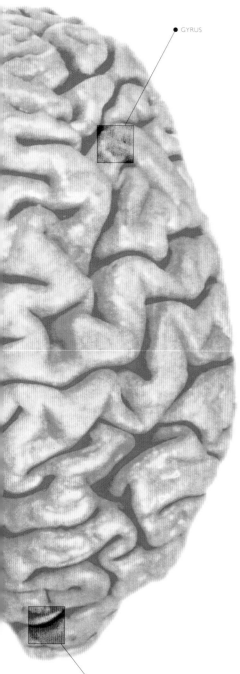

BELOW The surface of the human brain is grooved and corrugated – each groove is called a sulcus, and the corresponding bulge is known as a gyrus.

GYRUS

SULCUS

Drugs and the brain

One of the biggest questions in brain research today is how this plasticity might be important, not just in education and development of personality, but in compensating for an injury, such as a stroke. And if, as does happen, this quality of "plasticity" allows patients to make partial or even sometimes total recovery from brain damage, then why is there no such compensation in Alzheimer's disease and Parkinson's disease, where key brain cells slowly but inexorably die?

Brain research touches on other concerns of society, too. Take drugs. For the most part, drugs target the chemical transmitters in the brain and either increase or reduce their availability, or act as impostors, or block their actions. In this way it is possible to modify brain operations on a large scale, since drugs can have an effect in any part of the brain, wherever a particular chemical is at work. This is why it is impossible to have a drug without side effects – because the transmitters that are influenced by any particular drug will invariably be important in many brain functions.

But these considerations notwithstanding, some might dream of a drug, in the future, that is free from side effects and able simply to switch on a specific mood. We need to understand the full implications of drug action in the brain, to appreciate fully the ethical issues involved in allowing or denying individuals a chemical shortcut to peace of mind. If our personalities, our "minds," have evolved as our brain-cell connections have been built up through our experiences since birth, and if these connections work by means of chemical transmitters, and if chemical transmitters are modified by drugs, then the phrase "blowing the mind" could have a chilling accuracy.

Nonetheless, the study of drugs is currently helping us to understand how certain chemical events are directly related to certain feelings. Drugs could act, therefore, as a kind of Rosetta Stone for answering one of the big questions of the future – how the physical brain relates to the subjective inner state that we call the mind. However, even within the last ten years, we have seen yet another new approach to tackling these sorts of questions.

"Brain imaging" now, for the first time, offers us a window onto the conscious human brain at work. This technique exploits the fact that your brain is enormously greedy, consuming far more oxygen and glucose than any other part of your body at rest. By tagging the oxygen or glucose, or by monitoring any aspect of the brain as the blood flow carrying the oxygen and glucose changes, it has been possible, painlessly, to monitor the hardest-working parts of the brain during specific, and often very sophisticated, learning tasks.

Such studies have shown that there is no such thing as a "center" for different emotions, or for different brain functions such as memory, language, or vision. Instead, we now have direct proof that many brain regions work together in some kind of coordinated concert. Different constellations of different brain regions literally light up on the computer screen for the execution of different functions.

Yet some might fear that once we are able to relate brain structure to function more accurately, we will be tempted to manipulate the various areas of the brain. One sci-fi fantasy, for example, has been the implantation of silicon chips into the brain to simulate memory. Others think that, using the transplant process in reverse, eventually carbon could be downloaded onto silicon and the essence of a human being placed on a CD.

Science fiction and science fact

Even though such operations, at present, belong to the realm of scientific fantasy, awesome advances are occurring in the development of purely artificial devices. A silicon neuron has been constructed that can generate electrical signals in a fashion indistinguishable from its biological counterpart; and there is even a silicon retina that responds to visual stimulation, just like a real one. On a larger scale, robots are being developed that can

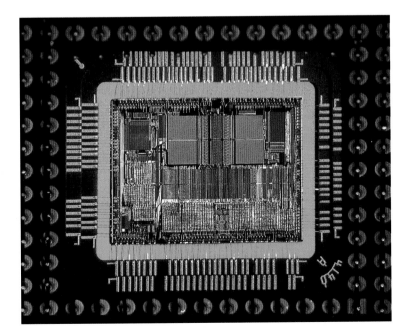

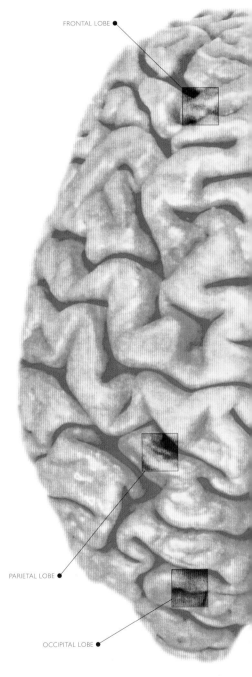

BELOW The pattern of corrugations that occurs is unique to each brain, but there are a few grooves that are common to everyone and are used as landmarks to distinguish different areas.

FRONTAL LOBE ●

PARIETAL LOBE ●

OCCIPITAL LOBE ●

LEFT The sci-fi fantasy of downloading a human brain onto some kind of digital media is unlikely to be realized.

learn and remember things in the kind of situations that confront a very small child. This type of study is, inevitably, provoking the question of whether such a machine could ever be "conscious."

Aside from far-fetched scenarios to do with silicon memories and brains on disk, there is the near certainty of the complete mapping of the human genome: of knowing what every gene in the human body is "for." A serious concern arising from this work – indeed a concern that is already with us – is that we will understand every human gene so well that we will be able to build custom-made people and to manipulate existing people by tinkering with their genes. With such ideas and speculation in the air, it is scarcely surprising that many people view the future of brain research with a certain suspicion.

BELOW Our brains grow and develop in accordance with our own personal experiences and lifestyles. This is what makes each brain unique and is the essence of our individuality.

ABOVE One of the fears that accompanies genetic research is that we will be tempted to try to create a super race of beautiful, intelligent, perfect people.

Things to come

Is the time coming when we will be able to manipulate the brain so precisely that we will effectively annihilate the individual? Such questions become increasingly relevant as we push back the frontiers of science. In this book we have set out to explain the latest thinking about how the brain works, enabling you to decide for yourself which scenarios are implausible and which require as much informed debate as possible.

On a humbler level, there are the implications of what we are currently doing with and to our brains. As we control our environment more and more, and as we bombard the brain with a vast array of in-your-face multimedia technology, is there a danger that the ability to retreat within one's mind, the familiar sense of losing yourself in the imagined world of a novel, for instance, will become a thing of the past? Perhaps the most immediate threat is not so much the hi-tech feat of creating conscious robots or genetically engineered minds as the banal reality of reduced attention span, loss of imagination and, hence, a decline in creativity.

We hope this book may provide insights that will help you to form judgments about issues such as these that will have an impact on the future of society. The six contributors from different areas of brain research have brought their own expertise to bear on some of these questions. We believe that knowing how your brain works – about what happens as you fall asleep, bring up your children, talk to your dog, cut your knee, listen to music, take drugs, and have sex – in itself enriches your life. Such is true brain power.

RIGHT Perhaps the most intrinsic and unique human quality is our ability to retreat into our own world of imagination, a world which no amount of computer simulation can reproduce.

The anatomy of your brain

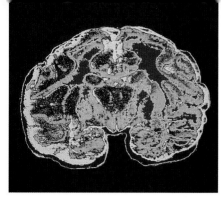

ABOVE The distinct brain hemispheres can be seen in this overhead scan.

*T*he human brain – your brain – is the most complicated structure in the known universe. It weighs just 44 ounces (1,250 grams) and is made of 100 billion nerve cells, known as neurons, connected together in an extraordinary degree of complexity. The nerve cells are surrounded by a further 1,000 billion cells, called glial cells, that form a supportive scaffolding – the glia (from the Greek for glue) – for the nerve cells, as well as performing many other functions, some of which are not fully understood.

Each of the nerve cells has a cell body, and from this body long rootlike fibers project. There are two kinds of fibers: **axons** and **dendrites**. Each nerve cell has one axon – along which it sends electrical impulses to other neurons – and a variable number of dendrites, which have many branches (indeed, down a microscope they look like the branches of a tree). Axons from other nerve cells are attached to the dendrites. The point of attachment is called a **synapse**. The dendrites receive electrical impulses from the attached axons and transmit them to the cell

MEDULLA

CORTEX

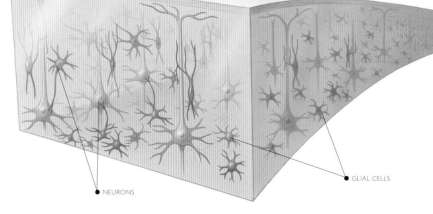

NEURONS

GLIAL CELLS

ABOVE The cortex is the convoluted surface layer of the brain and is made up of billions of cells. Glial cells hold the structure together, while neurons generate the brain's activity.

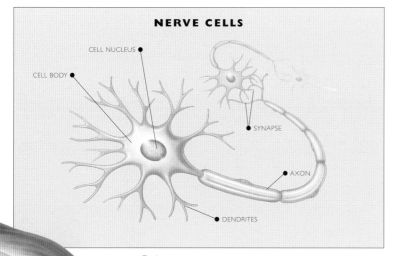

NERVE CELLS

CELL NUCLEUS

CELL BODY

SYNAPSE

AXON

DENDRITES

ABOVE Each nerve cell is made up of a body and a tail, the axon.

Depending on the balance of impulses received by an individual neuron's dendrites, the nerve cell may or may not be triggered into sending an impulse down its own axon to the dendrites of another nerve cell to which its own axon is attached. Each of the 100 billion nerve cells can be connected in this way to as many as 100,000 other nerve cells. Unimaginable complexity!

The nerves' cell bodies are packed together, and to the naked eye appear as the "gray matter" of the brain. They are organized into layered sheets, such as the **cerebral cortex**, into clumps called **nuclei**, and into netlike structures. When examined under a microscope, different areas of cerebral cortex have characteristically different architectural patterns. The axons – the "white matter" – are packed together to form major trunks or "fibertracts" connecting the cell bodies together. Nerve cells vary in size from 20 to 100 microns (millionths of a meter).

In the first few weeks of fetal life, the brain and spinal cord look like a hollow tube. As the fetus develops, the tube grows and one end of it expands, rather like a balloon, to form the brain. This "balloon" becomes thicker in some places than others; and because the human brain is so large relative to the size of the skull, it gets creased and folded – crumpled up like a ball of paper – in order to squeeze into the bony confines of the skull.

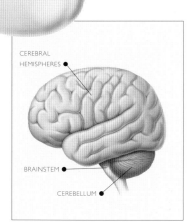

CEREBRAL HEMISPHERES

BRAINSTEM

CEREBELLUM

ABOVE The brain consists of three main sections, the cerebral hemispheres, the cerebellum, and the brainstem.

THE MAIN PARTS OF THE BRAIN

THE BRAIN is divided into three main parts: the cerebral hemispheres, the cerebellum, and the brainstem. In general terms, the **cerebral hemispheres** are where thinking, perceiving, and consciousness go on, whereas the **cerebellum** is responsible for the coordination of physical movement. The third part, the **brainstem**, is a kind of combined power station and telephone exchange for the cerebral hemispheres – relaying and modifying messages to and fro between the brain and the rest of the body, and also keeping the hemispheres awake and conscious.

The cerebral hemispheres consist of the folded and layered cortex of "gray matter" (the cell bodies) on the surface. This layer is what gives the brain its characteristic wrinkled appearance. Countless millions of axons beneath the cell bodies form the "deep white matter" of the brain. Underneath the cortex – buried in the deep white matter of the hemispheres – are a series of nuclei called the **basal ganglia**. A piece of brain the size of a pinhead contains approximately 60,000 nerve cells.

chapter one
in the genes

Like the rest of the body, the brain is made up
of cells, organized according to our own personal
genetic code. This first chapter offers a tour of the
brain and its component parts.

In the Genes

introduction

Listen to the cries of delight from the relatives clustering around any new baby. Invariably there will be claims that it has its father's nose or mother's eyes. Everyone knows that traits like these can be inherited. And as long ago as 1865 an Austrian monk, Gregor Mendel, showed how heritability conforms to a pattern, earning a place in history with his demonstration of the precise and predictable ratios in which peas would be yellow or green. But in those days no one really understood how such clear events came to pass. No one knew anything at all about what the package of information – a gene – really was, or how it worked.

The big breakthrough that started a revolution in how we think about life, and indeed how we now can manipulate and exploit forms of life, occurred at Cambridge University in the 1950s, when an American biologist, James Watson, joined forces with English physicist Francis Crick to discover the molecules and mechanism of inheritance. It was already suspected that the key lay in the nucleic

ABOVE Francis Crick and James Watson discovered the structure of the DNA molecule, the building block of life, for which they received the Nobel prize in 1962.

acid DNA. Using crucial X-ray data from crystallographer Rosalind Franklin, Crick and Watson were able to work out the structure of DNA – a double-stranded helical spiral – and to identify the critical chemical building blocks and mechanisms that enable a gene to pass on its code. This discovery opened up a new branch of science – molecular biology – and also added fuel to the ongoing controversy known as the "nature/nurture debate." To what extent are we the product of our genes, and to what extent are we molded by our own personal experiences?

ABOVE Genetic inheritance plays a part in determining what we are; the question is, how big a part?

Perhaps not surprisingly, the answer is that neither has absolute dominance: different forms of life are now recognized as a combined product of genes and the environment. Our genes are a recipe, but there are other factors that affect how that recipe will turn out. The big question is just how much each of these factors contributes. The most likely scenario is that it depends on the species. A goldfish, for example, acts out the dictates of its genes in a far more consistent and direct manner than do humans, who rely to a greater extent on learning gained through individual experience, rather than on "instinct."

ABOVE A primitive animal, such as a fish, is determined more completely by its genes than an animal with a more sophisticated way of life, such as a human being.

Finding the balance

In this chapter we shall explore exactly what we mean by instinct, and how the brains of sophisticated species who rely on learning differ from animals with a simpler agenda for life and a correspondingly narrower behavioral repertoire. But the powerful advances in molecular biology have also given rise to further difficult questions. For instance, is there a gene "for" homosexuality, or a gene that predisposes the individual to criminal behavior? Now that scientists can isolate genes and manipulate them, there is a growing school of thought that believes the brain and its workings can be reduced to specific genes. This obviously has important political implications for those who would like to exert control over society and conversely for those who might feel that they were being "victimized" because of their genes.

This first chapter examines what the brain is made of and how it is formed. We will look at the basic components of the brain and the way it is organized on different levels. We will investigate how we acquire and develop skills. And in the process, we shall explore how far everything about our personalities can be traced directly to our genes, and to what extent our brains bear the imprint of events in our individual lives.

RIGHT Our interactions with our families and our environment have an important role in the way our brains develop.

Nature vs. nurture

For millennia, philosophers have debated the extent to which human knowledge is predetermined. "Nativists," such as Plato (c. 428–348 B.C.E.), argued that all knowledge is derived from mathematical universals, and that these universals are the innate building blocks of everything we know or can know. "Empiricists," such as Aristotle (384–322 B.C.E.), on the other hand, argued that everything we know is a product of experience – no amount of verbal description could convey the beauty of a rose to a person blind from birth.

The debate continues to this day, particularly among philosophers, psychologists, and linguists attempting to explain the higher levels of cognitive functioning, such as memory, language, and perception. Most scientists now agree that the capacity for high-level mental processing is inherited. There is disagreement, however, about exactly what is inherited. Those in the nativist tradition tend to argue that our genetic inheritance provides us with a great deal of specific knowledge about the world. They would claim that we come into the world knowing that most objects are solid, that they move around the world in a continuous fashion, and don't cease to exist when they disappear from sight. In contrast, latter-day empiricists maintain that brain systems do not come equipped with specific knowledge but with the capacity to acquire knowledge, often at a phenomenal rate. They also stress that the acquisition of knowledge depends on the right environmental stimulation. On this view, if we grew up in a world of virtual reality where apparently solid objects could pass through each other or suddenly change position, our reasoning about the world around us would be radically different. The debate is no longer about whether nature or nurture is the fount of knowledge, but the extent to which each contributes to the human condition and how they work together to create a unique individual.

LEFT Plato believed that everything we know is built up, like a child's construction toy, from a universal store of specific inherited items.

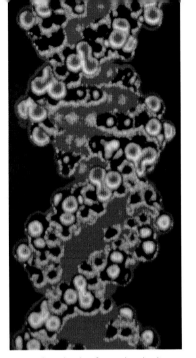

ABOVE A molecule of DNA, showing its characteristic helical shape. DNA is the material from which genes are made, and our genes constitute the "recipe" that determines, to some extent, how our bodies and brains develop.

BELOW Our environment plays as much a part in our mental development as our inheritance – the place where we live, the people we live with, even the TV programs we watch.

THE INFLUENCE OF GENES

EACH HUMAN GENE provides a unique template for manufacturing a chain of amino acids. These gene products are called proteins or (if they are relatively small) peptides. Proteins come in endlessly different configurations and perform diverse functions – as enzymes, as building blocks for cells, and as neurotransmitters. Thus, asserting that a particular gene is responsible for a complex human trait (for example, homosexuality, an extrovert personality, alcoholism, or criminality) is like claiming that the character of a symphony depends on information contained in just one particular chord. Such a claim is obviously simplistic, and yet the chord in question may indeed play a crucial role in the symphony's structure and impact.

Before birth, as the embryo develops, cells specialize and migrate to their final site in the body – where each employs only a small part of the complete set of genes it contains. In fact, the effect of a particular gene may be completely different at a different site in the body. For example, a previously undiscovered peptide was found to cause contractions in the gall bladder. However, the same peptide was subsequently detected at various sites in the brain, where it appeared to be linked to a whole range of conditions, including analgesia, schizophrenia, and the suppression of hunger.

INHERITED TIMING

Any theory proposing a simple relationship between a specific gene and a particular form of behavior requires cautious appraisal. Nevertheless, recent studies have shown that certain fundamental processes can sometimes be influenced by a single gene. A remarkable example concerns the clock in the brain that governs our daily lives (see pages 100-101). Great excitement was generated a few years ago by the discovery of a hamster with a 20-hour body clock, instead of the usual 24-hour one. When it bred with a normal hamster, some of the offspring exhibited a 20-hour rhythm in their exercise routine, while some retained the standard 24-hour rhythm and others displayed a 22-hour cycle. By analyzing the proportion of offspring with these different traits, it was shown that just a single gene was responsible for them. This unexpected example of the power of a single gene suggests that our understanding of biology is still far too primitive to permit reliable generalizations about "nature versus nurture."

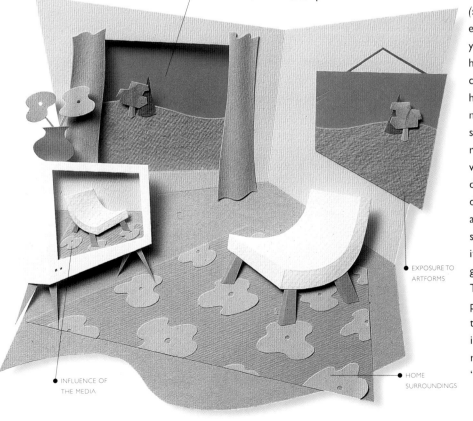

EXPERIENCE OF NATURE

EXPOSURE TO ARTFORMS

HOME SURROUNDINGS

INFLUENCE OF THE MEDIA

Skill development

*A*lthough it is true that the basic anatomical structure of the human brain is common to all of us, the details of the microcircuitry vary subtly from one individual to the next. For example, the precise cortical areas of the brain that are responsible for motor control are not wired up in exactly the same way for everyone.

ABOVE From the moment we are born, our brains begin to grow and change in ways that are unique to each one of us and make us different from the crowd.

The human brain is fairly flexible in the solutions it finds for everyday problems, such as picking up an object. If you lose a finger, you need to find new ways to manipulate objects; the brain accommodates such changes by reorganizing the synapses between the neurons responsible for control of the fingers.

The plasticity of the brain enables it to develop through learning, which in turn means that individuals can benefit from experience. This is particularly useful if you want to acquire a complicated skill. For example, when learning to talk, you don't need to know all the words in a language before starting to communicate: you can rely on your environment to provide you with additional vocabulary and grammar. It is true that you need to be good at recognizing words, but even very young infants seem preadapted to achieve this.

BELOW Human brains are peculiarly well-adapted to learning new and difficult skills because of the quality of plasticity, the capacity to adapt as a result of experience.

RIGHT The interlocking hexagons of a beehive have nothing to do with the design skills of the bees. The honey cells start off as cylinders, and the pressure of the bees pushing one cell outward against its neighbor produces the hexagonal shapes.

PRIMITIVE SPECIES, such as worms, do not derive much benefit from learning. Because they have a simple nervous system, they can only display a limited repertoire of behaviors, such as reacting to changes in light or moisture. So experience has little effect on their structure or behavior. However, even very simple creatures show an ability to learn and to remember, allowing them to adapt to their environments. For example, slugs are able to learn that particular odors are associated with unpleasant tastes. This is of considerable importance for an animal that finds food primarily by smell and can't move very fast: think of the time saved if it can learn that certain smells are not worth investigating. But the learning abilities of such primitive animals are limited, and even among most mammals it is unlikely that memory recall implies the kinds of recollection that humans experience.

Some animal species display behavior that appears to be complex. Have you ever marveled at the intricate pattern of the honeycombs in a beehive? The perfection and intricacy of the design suggests that a complex skill has been mastered by bees – but that is not in fact the case. Initially, the honey cells are cylindrical, but the wax walls undergo deformation because the bees knead the wax to create as much space as possible within each cell. Since each cell abuts six others, the surface tension of the wax and the "packing pressure" exerted by the bees combine to force each cylinder into a hexagonal shape. The hexagonal shape maximizes both the number of cells that can be packed into the hive and the volume of each cell, thus making the most economical use of the bees' wax. The labor of the bees and the forces of physics collude with each other to produce the hexagonal shape of the honey cells. Bees don't need to know anything about hexagons.

RIGHT A work of art such as Michelangelo's David is a supreme example of the sophisticated skills that human beings can acquire.

Human learning

In humans, the majority of complex skills have to be acquired through a protracted period of development. It is arguable that evolution has made us relatively helpless at birth so we can maximize both our genetic inheritance and the opportunities for learning available from the environment in which we live. An adult human is much more than the sum of the building blocks of nature and nurture. When hydrogen and oxygen combine to produce water, they create a compound with properties quite different from its constituent elements; similarly, nature and nurture interact to yield a product that is not entirely predictable from its origins. The complexity of the human brain is in itself the supreme demonstration of what can be achieved through the interaction of nature and nurture.

Instinct vs. learning

Learning something is a matter of acquiring experience of the world in which we live. We may learn facts and skills through an explicit educational process, or pick things up without consciously realizing we are doing so – such as avoiding situations that are unpleasant or threatening. Either way, learning involves adjusting synaptic connections between neurons in the brain. As far as we know, both factual and practical knowledge are retained in the brain as patterns of connectivity that can trigger patterns of activity when we access that information. So learning must involve changes in the pathways that control the flow of neural energy.

Instincts are innate abilities that require minimal triggering by the environment. For example, a newborn foal is able to walk without learning to do so. Neuronal pathways are already laid down that provide the basis for the complex motor coordinations underlying its initial attempts to move around. This knowledge about how to walk has been preprogrammed to show itself at birth. Experience may "tune" the neurons to make the foal a more efficient walker, but evolution has "orchestrated" the broad sweep of its initial capabilities.

Following our instincts

We generally assume that animals are driven by instinct, whereas human behavior is shaped by the culture in which we live. Both assumptions are broadly true, but underestimate the degree to which human behavior is instinct-driven and the behavior of animals shaped by the environment in which they live. We tend to think of instinct as synonymous with primitive behavior. But quite complicated abilities in humans can be instinctual, or at least do not seem to be learned. For example, newborn human infants exhibit an innate preference for looking at visual stimuli that resemble the human face. This makes good sense from an evolutionary perspective, because a preference for human faces is likely to enhance an infant's chances of establishing and maintaining contact with a care giver, thereby increasing its chances of survival. However, the ability to recognize human faces is not entirely determined at birth. Only part of this skill is instinctual, some of it is learned. If newborn babies are presented with schematic outlines of faces, they prefer to look at an outline where a few simple features – such as the eyes and nose – are in the appropriate position, rather than an outline where these features are jumbled up. But they don't prefer to look at cartoon faces rather than real faces. It is as if babies are born with the instinct to look for objects that have some of the basic properties of faces, but need to experience these objects in order to learn what a face really looks like. Instinct prompts the infant to look in the right direction. Learning takes care of the rest.

How we learn

This trade-off between instinct and learning is the rule rather than the exception. Very few skills are entirely instinctual except in the most simple organisms. Likewise, there are no behaviors that are entirely learned. All new skills rely on existing abilities: some learned, some instinctual. We can only learn to play chess if we already understand the concept of playing a game, of winning and losing, of moving a piece, of turn-taking, etc. Learning is a process of building on our current state of knowledge.

ABOVE Learning to play chess is only partly a matter of being told the rules and practicing. You also need to have a basic concept of what a game is and what winning means, ideas that you acquire rather than being taught.

FAR LEFT Babies have a kind of innate blueprint for some of the skills that they learn, such as walking and recognizing faces. These skills develop with experience, but there is already an instinctive template in place at birth.

BASIC INSTINCTS

It is possible to observe instinctual human behavior by looking at a newborn baby. If the baby is held upright over a surface, it will move its legs as if to walk (even though of course its legs are not strong enough to bear its weight). Similarly, a newborn baby will automatically suck if it is offered a breast or bottle (although even in this case the baby has to learn to suck in a way that makes the milk flow efficiently).

Levels of the brain

A central theme of this book is that we cannot fully "understand" the brain by examining it from just one perspective. There are many levels at which the brain can be understood – at the level of genetics, of molecular biochemistry, of cells, of neural networks, of neurological processes, and finally of thoughts and feelings.

In technical terms, the brain is organized into a hierarchy of levels. Consequently, a hierarchy of languages is needed to explain it. We can describe emotions, for instance, in terms of chemical changes in certain parts of the brain, but it is important not to confuse description with explanation. It would appear that people who are depressed have low levels of the chemical serotonin in certain parts of their brain, but it doesn't follow that lack of serotonin is the cause of their depression. On the other hand, it is equally inappropriate to talk about emotions without any reference to their existence as physical events inside the brain.

For each level of the brain's organization, a different set of questions and answers about structure and function is appropriate. In discussing the brain's organization, neuroscientists sometimes use the analogy of a house. It is of little value, for instance, to answer a question about the arrangement of the walls of a bedroom by describing the clay used to make the bricks in the walls. In broader terms, imagine trying to describe a house to someone from Mars without being allowed to make any reference to the fact that human beings live in it. And how could you convey the nature of a kitchen, dining room, or bedroom without saying that they are used for cooking, eating, and sleeping?

ABOVE A brain is like a house in the sense that both are organized in particular ways for particular functions, and both can be examined at different levels.

LEFT Happiness can be described as a series of chemical reactions in the brain, but that does not give much idea of why a person might be happy. It is as important to be aware of the context of the physical changes as of the changes themselves.

OVERALL FUNCTION IS
A COMBINATION OF
STRUCTURE AND USE ●

UPPORTING
TRUCTURE ●

DIFFERENT AREAS
FOR DIFFERENT
FUNCTIONS

NFORMATION COMES
N FROM OUTSIDE ●

HOW THE BRAIN IS ORGANIZED

Genes and chemicals

These are the basic materials of which the brain is composed. They are equivalent to the particles of clay from which the bricks of a house are made.

Cells and synapses

Using the house analogy, the cells are the bricks or building blocks. The synapses are the equivalent of the joints between them.

Circuits

The neurons (nerve cells) are linked together to form circuits, just as the bricks are joined together to form walls.

Networks

The circuits of connected neurons are joined together to form neural networks – in roughly the same way that the walls are joined together to form the rooms of a house.

Regions

The rooms of a house are arranged into different areas – upstairs and downstairs, for example – just as the brain is organized into regions, such as the cerebellum and the cerebral hemispheres.

Systems

Just as the floors of a house are organized into rooms that have different sorts of furniture in them, so the neural networks are grouped into systems that have different functions.

The overall function

The "function" of a house cannot be understood without reference to the lives of the people who live in it. Similarly, the brain cannot be understood solely by talking about cells and neural networks.

Genes and chemicals

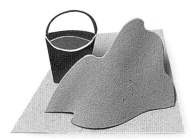

ABOVE Genes and chemicals are the first components required in building the brain, like the sand and cement from which the house begins.

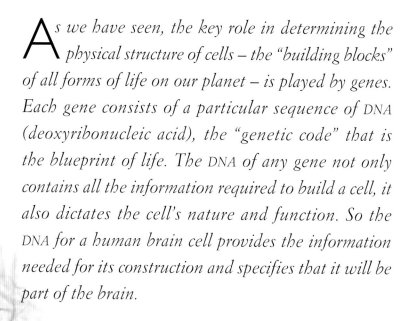

As we have seen, the key role in determining the physical structure of cells – the "building blocks" of all forms of life on our planet – is played by genes. Each gene consists of a particular sequence of DNA (deoxyribonucleic acid), the "genetic code" that is the blueprint of life. The DNA of any gene not only contains all the information required to build a cell, it also dictates the cell's nature and function. So the DNA for a human brain cell provides the information needed for its construction and specifies that it will be part of the brain.

In human beings, each gene encodes the information required to produce – or, in genetic terminology, "express" – one particular protein. A protein is made up of a chain of chemicals called amino acids, of which there are twenty different types. The characteristics of a particular protein are determined by the specific amino-acid sequence that makes it up, and by the three-dimensional structure that its chain of amino acids takes up.

With a few exceptions, proteins are the only biologically active components of a cell, so they are vital to the control of all aspects of its life. These include its assembly, the way it functions (that is, whether it becomes a skin cell or a blood cell or a brain cell), and any long-term changes in its nature. Protein expression is increased, decreased, and switched on and off by interaction between various molecules – most of them themselves proteins – and the genes. The state of a cell is therefore a continually evolving reflection of the spectrum of genes that are being expressed as proteins.

LEFT A light micrograph of a section of the brain's gray matter, showing the brown nerve cells with their dendrites and axons, and the smaller purple glial cells that form the supporting structure.

HOW CELLS COMMUNICATE

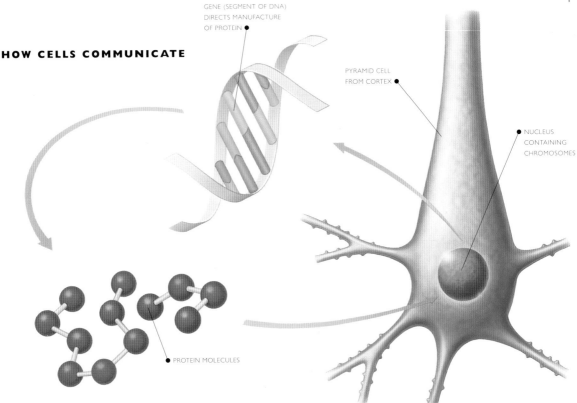

GENE (SEGMENT OF DNA)
DIRECTS MANUFACTURE
OF PROTEIN

PYRAMID CELL
FROM CORTEX

NUCLEUS
CONTAINING
CHROMOSOMES

PROTEIN MOLECULES

NEUROTRANSMITTER MOLECULES

THE ABILITY TO TRANSMIT and receive signals is vital to all cells, but it is particularly important to those in the central nervous system. A cell usually conveys information to other cells by releasing a chemical molecule as a transmitter; in the central nervous system these molecules are known as neurotransmitters. They come in many shapes and sizes, and from more than one family of chemicals. In fact, the variety of different molecules involved in neurotransmission is staggering.

The information carried by a neurotransmitter often has nothing to do with its chemical structure. Instead, it lies in the release pattern of the transmitter, both in isolation and in conjunction with the release patterns of other transmitters.

The transmission of information between cells works as follows. The receiving cell recognizes the arrival of a transmitter molecule when it interacts with a receptor, a protein that normally lies on the outer surface of the cell. The interaction is then translated into a signal within the cell. Each receptor is specific for a particular molecule, so a cell needs to be equipped with a variety of receptors. However, although most neurotransmitters are recognized by more than one type of receptor, each with its own mode of response, a cell may not have every type. The responsiveness of a cell to any one of the various chemicals that may come into contact with it is therefore determined by the range of receptors that it displays.

ABOVE Genes act as a code that produces a particular protein. Proteins are the active part of cells, governing their construction, their function, and any changes that occur within them.

IMPORTANT NEUROTRANSMITTERS

Neurotransmitters are divided up into families on the basis of their biochemical structure. Some of the most important neurotransmitters are listed below.

GABA	the most widespread inhibitory neurotransmitter
glutamate	the major excitatory transmitter
acetylcholine	transmits nervous impulses to muscles, important for learning and memory
noradrenalin	excitatory chemical causing mental and physical arousal
dopamine	important for stimulating movement
serotonin	part of the brain's "reward" system, produces feelings of pleasure
endorphins	produce pain-killing effects

Cells and synapses

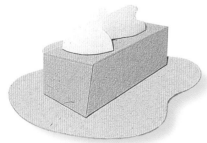

*N*eurons have a unique form that reflects their function. Like other cells, each neuron has a cell body, but here the physical similarity ends. As described in the section outlining the anatomy of the brain, at one end of the neuron lies a long thin structure that extends from the cell body toward other neurons; this is the axon, the main output pathway of the cell. From the opposite end of the cell body extends a treelike array of dendrites; these are the cell's input antennae.

Unlike most other types of cell, neurons are electrically active. In fact, they are capable of transmitting electrical impulses along the entire length of their structure. Any information received by the dendrites is integrated by the cell body, which then initiates an electrical impulse at the "axon hillock," the part of the cell where the axon is joined to the cell body. From here, it travels along the entire length of the axon until it reaches the filigree of termini that sprout from the end of the axon.

Transmitting the signal

At this point, the impulse needs to be transmitted to the cell that is to receive it. Neurons do this in one of two ways. In some cases, two neurons form what is known as a gap-junction – a protein bridge between the two cells that places the intracellular content of the one cell in direct contact with that of the other. In terms of the conduction of the electrical impulse, the second cell in effect becomes a direct continuation of the first.

By far the most important type of junction, however, relies on chemical transmission, which takes the form of a specialized link between the two cells called a synapse. At a synapse the

DENDRITE

CELL BODY

AXON

ABOVE Nerve cells in the cerebral cortex, magnified 170 times. The nerve cells are arranged in a variable number of layers to form the cerebral cortex.

membranes of the two cells lie close together, although there is no direct connection between the cell contents. This is where the neurotransmitters come into play, by forming a "chemical bridge" between the two cells. Each neurotransmitter is released into the fluid of the synapse by the "presynaptic" neuron, and recognized by a receptor on the "postsynaptic" neuron. The response of the receptor then determines the effect on the postsynaptic neuron.

Unlike the electrical transmission effected by a gap-junction, which faithfully conducts the signal from one cell to the next, synaptic chemical transmission is not inevitable. This is because a single impulse from the transmitting cell may not release enough neurotransmitter to induce an impulse in the receiving neuron. Indeed, it often takes many convergent inputs on many different dendrites to trigger an impulse. So the cell body has to integrate the many signals that arrive at the neuron from a variety of sources. Synaptic transmission contributes in no small measure to the brain's complexity. It is also the target of almost all psychoactive drugs.

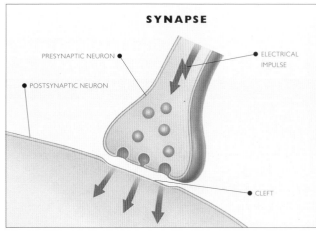

SYNAPSE

PRESYNAPTIC NEURON

POSTSYNAPTIC NEURON

ELECTRICAL IMPULSE

CLEFT

ABOVE The most important type of cell junction is the synapse. This is a fluid-filled gap between two cells, and messages are passed between the cells by chemicals called neurotransmitters.

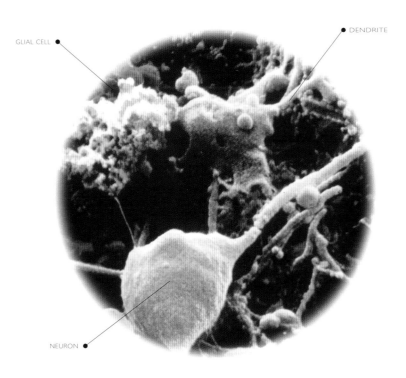

GLIAL CELL

DENDRITE

NEURON

ABOVE A colored scanning electron micrograph showing glial cells and neurons, magnified 1700 times. The small tubelike structures are dendrites.

ELECTRICAL TRANSMISSION

When a neurotransmitter arrives at the relevant receptor after crossing the synaptic cleft, it causes a change in the chemical structure of the receptor. This results in "holes" appearing in the outer membrane of the nerve cell through which negatively or positively charged particles (called ions) can pass. Ions can move out from the cell or into the cell. The direction of movement depends on the kind of charge (positive or negative) that the ion is carrying, and the prevailing electric field across the cell membrane. This movement of charged ions across the cell membrane is what produces an impulse in the postsynaptic neuron.

Circuits

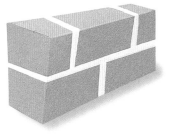

ABOVE Nerve cells are linked in circuits, like the walls of a house, which perform particular functions and operations within the brain.

*A*lthough the brain is made up of individual neurons, none of them work as individuals: they all constantly interact with other neurons. So what each cell does depends on what the cells that it is connected to are doing. Activity in a neuron changes in response to the activity of the other cells that are its inputs; these changes in turn determine the signals the neuron sends to its own output targets, some of which may even send inputs back to the cell we started with. The connections that cells have – the circuits they are in – are therefore of crucial importance.

There are many specialized circuits. Some deal with the senses: the visual circuits deal with aspects of what we see (such as movement, shape, or color) in different specialized modules, so that damage to different areas of the brain leads to different visual impairments. For example, carbon-monoxide poisoning occasionally leads to loss of color vision, while leaving face perceptions unaffected. Furthermore, people who have lost their color vision in this way find they can no longer imagine or remember color, even though they lived in a world of color before they were poisoned. It would therefore appear that the brain systems needed for seeing in color are also needed for thinking about it.

Other circuits deal with memory. Again, selective damage destroys only part of the normal function. People with damage to the area of the brain known as the hippocampus *(see pages 36–7)* often cannot remember from minute to minute what has happened each day, but they may remember very clearly things that happened many years previously. The reason is that different bits of each circuit make their own special contribution to the function of the whole.

LEFT Circuits are divided into specialized modules; for example color is dealt with by one area of the vision circuit while movement is dealt with by another.

ORANGE

YELLOW

RED

BELOW The basic brain circuit that controls movement is created automatically, but the gracefulness of a dancer's movements will be reflected in the complexity of her movement circuitry.

How circuits are connected up

How do neurons know which cells to connect up to? Much of the circuitry of the brain is preprogrammed by our genes, in much the same way that the cells were instructed to become brain cells in the first place. When the brain develops, neurons grow connections out toward the appropriate targets. If brain cells have mutated as a result of an error in their genetic code, the signals guiding the connections don't work properly, and the right pattern of circuits never develops. This will result in abnormal behavior or some type of deficiency; for instance, a person might have a poor memory, or be unable to walk straight, or be unable to speak properly.

However, although our genes play a vitally important role in setting up our brain circuits, our experiences influence the way they develop. Cells compete for their places in the circuits. Connections that work well get stronger, at the expense of weaker connections, whose cells may eventually die in a programmed suicide. Thus, although the general layout of our brain circuits may be programmed by our evolutionary history, so that cells in visual circuits or in memory circuits know where they should grow to, the final pattern depends on our own interactions with the world around us. Here again is an aspect of the brain's plasticity: if we are exposed to particular kinds of stimuli (for instance if we grow up in a musical environment, or we are encouraged to play ball games) the relevant connections in our brains will become stronger. Our own brain circuits are tuned to our own particular world.

"GLOBAL" AND "SERIAL" NEURONS

SOME OF THE MOST IMPORTANT CIRCUITS in the brain are those that consist of "global" neurons. These release one of five neurotransmitters: acetylcholine, noradrenalin, dopamine, 5-hydroxy-tryptamine (5-HT), and histamine. The cell bodies of these neurons are situated in discrete cell groups in areas of the central nervous system concerned with relatively low-level functions. However, although there are not very many of them, they branch to such an extent that their axon terminals make connections with large areas of the brain (hence their name).

Acting over a relatively long time scale, these cell groups influence the flow of information between the "serial" neurons – the cells that form the fast synaptic networks responsible for the higher-level processing and output of the brain. The neurotransmitters of the global neurons facilitate transmission between neurons, but do not instigate any action themselves. Consequently, they have been said to "energize" the brain. This concept helps explain Parkinson's disease, in which the loss of a particular group of these neurons – the dopamine-containing neurons of the area called the substantia nigra (see pages 140–1) – limits the brain's ability to initiate motor movements.

Networks

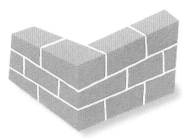

Nerve cells interconnect in a maze of identifiable sub-systems called neural networks. Some networks are small and localized; others involve very large numbers of neurons and are distributed diffusely over wide regions of the brain. A network often has a particular task to carry out. For example, the hippocampus is involved in helping to memorize experiences, including faces or names. We know this because patients who have suffered damage to the hippocampus, either through accident or surgery, can retrieve old memories, but have difficulty storing new experiences in their long-term memory.

The manner in which the neurons are connected together in the hippocampus makes it particularly well suited to this task. The activity in each neuron is passed to other neurons in a "reverberating loop" of connections, so that the activity of any individual neuron is influenced by the activity of many other neurons. Eventually, this reverberating activity settles into a stable pattern that corresponds to the brain's identification of a particular memory. The high level of interconnectivity in this network is good for building memory traces because it can combine information from many different sources (taste, smell, sound, vision) to create a composite pattern of activity that is unique to a particular experience.

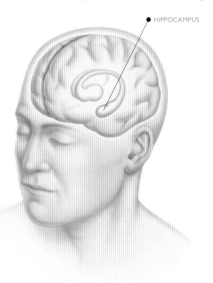

HIPPOCAMPUS

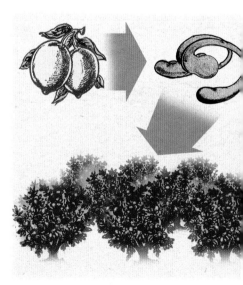

ABOVE The way the hippocampus is linked up to other parts of the brain means that it is able to retrieve a complete scene or episode from one remembered fragment, a smell or a taste or a piece of music.

LEFT The hippocampus is situated between the cerebral hemispheres; its name is the Greek word for seahorse because of its resemblance to the animal.

What is more, this type of network can reconstruct a memory from just a fragment of the original material. Once a memory pattern has been established and stored, it can be accessed by

ABOVE Different types of networks can perform different operations. A network that recalls a scene from the past will not be the same as a network that remembers how to ride a bicycle.

BELOW Computer simulations are helping scientists to understand how neural networks develop in children.

any one of the separate elements that made up the original scene or experience. A specific instance of this is our remembering of people. Hearing a person's voice can help conjure up their name or appearance. This is because there is a network of neurons where many of the characteristics that define a person are molded together into a single, unique experience. Exposure to just one of these characteristics can trigger a memory of the whole person.

NETWORK ARCHITECTURE

ONE OF THE MAJOR TASKS confronting brain scientists today is to understand how neural networks function. We know that subtle differences in the architecture of a network can have a massive impact on their capacity to perform different tasks. For example, networks that lack feedback connections have considerable difficulty distinguishing events that occur at different times. Sometimes, this isn't a problem. You might only want to know that something happened, not when it happened. More often than not, however, timing is critical; for example, you need to put the clothes into your washing machine before switching it on, and not vice versa.

A common technique used to understand brain networks better is to simulate them on a computer: by creating models of parts of the brain, scientists can investigate how artificial neural networks function. The advantage of using computers is that it is possible to tinker with different parts of the network to see how changing it, or removing them, can affect its function. This offers insights that cannot, because of the practical difficulties, be achieved by studying real human brains. It is even possible to "train" artificial networks on a computer and investigate how neural networks develop in infants and children.

Regions

ABOVE At the highest level of organization, the brain can be divided into regions, like the upstairs and downstairs of a house. The three main brain regions are the cerebral hemispheres, the brainstem, and the cerebellum.

W e have now reached the macro-level of organization in the brain, the regional level. Study of the microscopic structures of the brain shows what it is made of and how it is connected up. Studying at the level of regions begins to reveal the way the brain performs its various functions, and how responsibility for these activities is distributed among the different areas. Correspondingly, this level of enquiry also shows the kinds of things that can go wrong.

The human brain's extraordinary complexity, achieved through millions of years of vertebrate evolution, is reflected in its structure. The spinal cord is similar to that of a fish, while the midbrain resembles that of a cat, and the primary sensory and motor areas in the cerebral cortex are much like those of a monkey. But the highest levels of all, the "association areas" of the temporal, parietal, and frontal cortex, are found only in humans. These association areas collate the information processed by the different sensory systems and then compare this information with stored memories and evaluate it in relation to biological drives, emotions, and likely outcomes. In other words, they are where our conscious thought processes occur and where we make our decisions.

The brain's development in the embryo recalls its evolution: a single layer of neural stem cells is gradually built upon to form

BELOW The brains of other animals have features in common with the human brain, but the degree of complexity of our brains is found in no other animal.

FISH BRAIN

CAT BRAIN

MONKEY BRAIN

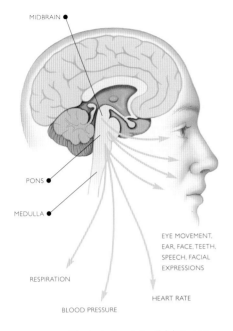

MIDBRAIN ●

PONS ●

MEDULLA ●

EYE MOVEMENT,
EAR, FACE, TEETH,
SPEECH, FACIAL
EXPRESSIONS

RESPIRATION

BLOOD PRESSURE

HEART RATE

ABOVE The brainstem is the link between the brain and the spinal cord, and it also controls a range of facial movements.

BELOW The human brain is much larger than the brains of other animals. This size difference is concentrated in the cortex and neocortex, the areas associated with planning, organization, and language.

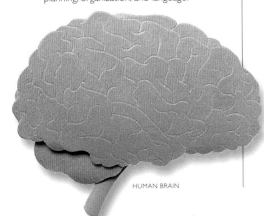

HUMAN BRAIN

the completed structure. A sequence of genes is switched on that causes the coordinated division of wave after wave of cells. These migrate to their final positions, creating the laminated structures of the spinal cord, the cerebral cortex, and the cerebellar cortex. Meanwhile, nerve cells in the brainstem clump into "nuclei" that specialize in different processing functions.

The processing operations that each brain region can carry out are determined by its neuronal architecture. Each area of the cerebral cortex, for example, analyzes a relatively small number of mainly local inputs. In contrast, the hippocampus and cerebellum process inputs from widely different sources. They use the results of these operations to control the functioning of the glands and muscles.

THE EFFECTS OF BRAIN DAMAGE

DAMAGE TO DIFFERENT AREAS of the brain results in different problems. If somebody suffers a major stroke, caused by one of the major arteries to the brain being blocked, an entire brain region can stop working. The left cerebral hemisphere, for instance, is responsible for controlling the right side of the body and also, in the majority of people, for language and calculation. So if the left middle cerebral artery becomes blocked, the ability to talk or to understand speech is lost, and the right arm and leg will be paralyzed. Conversely, the right cerebral hemisphere is responsible for the left side of the body, and also for understanding three-dimensional problems such as pulling on a sweater or finding your way around your home. People who experience a major right-sided stroke may therefore have problems with dressing themselves or get lost in familiar places, as well as suffering paralysis of the left arm and left leg.

The cerebellum is involved in coordinating movement, so damage to the cerebellum causes clumsy and uncoordinated movement. As a result, those who have suffered such damage are sometimes thought to be drunk by people unaware of their condition.

The brainstem connects the higher areas of the brain to the spinal cord and keeps these higher areas awake. It also contains nuclei for controlling the muscles responsible for swallowing, facial sensation, and moving the eyes. If the brainstem is damaged, profound coma or paralysis may occur, or a complicated range of difficulties with swallowing or eye movement. The brainstem also generates the rhythmic nerve impulses that make us breathe.

Direct damage to the brainstem – as happens when people attempt suicide by shooting themselves through the mouth – is often immediately fatal, whereas direct damage to the cerebral hemispheres or cerebellum will not in itself cause death. However, extensive damage to these regions does produce severe swelling of the injured parts, which increases the pressure inside the skull. As a result, the brainstem stops working, because the increased pressure in the head makes it difficult for the heart to supply the brain with blood, and breathing then ceases.

Systems

"Thoughts are but movements confined to the brain," wrote Sir Charles Sherrington, who was one of the first pioneers of neuroscience and won the Nobel Prize for his analysis of the basic processing operations carried out by the spinal cord. From the point of view of survival, which is the driving force of evolution, the main purpose of the brain is to control movement, to decide the best set of actions to deal with a situation. Consciousness itself probably evolved in order to make this process more efficient.

Movement

Everything to do with movement starts in the frontal lobe of the cerebral cortex, while everything to do with sensation takes place in the back half of the cerebral cortex, in the temporal, parietal, and occipital lobes. Conscious perception – the interpretation of sensory input – requires interaction between the front and back parts, and so does movement.

All movements are controlled through three main pathways. The direct cortical route consists of fibers that link the back of the cortex with the motor cortex in the frontal lobe. These are responsible for conscious control. Most movements are automatic, however, and are triggered through two much bigger indirect subcortical pathways. The first travels through the basal ganglia within each cerebral hemisphere, which help select the best motor program for the job. The second, larger, subcortical pathway travels through the cerebellum, which uses sensory inputs and information about the success of movements in the past to refine their execution in the future.

Internal drives such as hunger, thirst, self-preservation, and sex activate whichever pathway is appropriate. The motor programs themselves – the sequences of signals that switch on the right muscles at the right time – are generated by the motor cortex, brainstem, and spinal cord.

LEFT It is possible to identify specific pathways through the brain that act like major highways, carrying information.

ABOVE Like a central processing system, the brain performs a range of automatic functions to keep our bodies in a balanced state.

BELOW Three main pathways through the brain control movement. Motor control is associated with two areas at the top of the cortex.

MEMORY

OUR OWN INDIVIDUAL EXPERIENCES are stored as memories. The ability to recollect our past not only gives us much of our sense of personal identity, it also gives us the capacity to change our behavior as a result of experience. The brain systems that underlie normal memory in humans seem to do so in other mammals, too; the information we store may be more abstract and more complex, but the mechanisms of storage are probably identical. Although the neocortex, the most recent part of the brain to have evolved, seems to play a part in some aspects of memory, the really key systems are not there but in older structures, such as the hippocampus, buried deep under the neocortex in the temporal lobes. Damage to this structure, or to its key inputs and outputs, whether caused by lack of oxygen, by accident or by disease (including Alzheimer's), produces a devastating loss of memory.

Regulatory mechanisms

The widely held belief that the brain is dedicated to thinking, feeling, remembering, and moving, and not much else, does its scope an injustice and shows how little we can depend on conscious experience when trying to assess what our brains are "doing." The brain also incorporates a vast range of "autonomic" systems – systems over which we have no voluntary control and of which we may have little or no awareness. Many of these systems are dedicated to keeping bodily functions in balance. Their action is similar to that of a thermostat regulating the central heating in a building: when the temperature is too low, the boiler is activated until the set level is reached. Similar controls are required to regulate blood glucose and blood pressure. The broad term for such processes is homeostasis (from Greek, meaning "maintaining the same state"). It is now clear that the processes in question do not merely respond to an acute crisis. The equilibrium of our bodies would be poorly maintained if we always waited for dehydration before drinking – an ability to predict and prepare is vital for efficient regulation (*see pages 86–7 and 100–101*).

THE MAIN MOTOR PATHWAYS

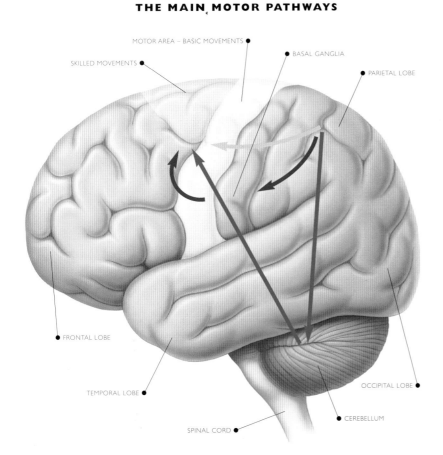

MOTOR AREA – BASIC MOVEMENTS

SKILLED MOVEMENTS

BASAL GANGLIA

PARIETAL LOBE

FRONTAL LOBE

TEMPORAL LOBE

OCCIPITAL LOBE

CEREBELLUM

SPINAL CORD

The overall function

ABOVE The completed house becomes a living space. In the same way, the brain as a whole has to be related to the person who uses it.

A central theme of this book is that although the brain has specialized regions that perform different functions, it has to be seen as an integrated whole. That this is so is suggested by the way in which the various brain regions have such extensive interconnections with each other.

What, then, is the overall function of the brain? A commonsense answer would be that the brain is closely identified with the "self" – that it is the center of our consciousness, and of our ability to make decisions and moral choices. However, many neuroscientists have some difficulty with such a view. Instead, they see the brain as a series of "modules" developed by evolution to solve the specific problems of survival and reproduction that our ancestors have been faced with over a huge period of time. The brain, they argue, is a machine (although admittedly a very complicated one), and consciousness and "free will" are illusions or "epiphenomena": our conscious self is like a sailor in a storm who points the rudder of his boat in the direction forced upon him by the wind, then claims to be steering the boat in that direction of his own free choice. This analogy was first suggested by the ancient Greek writer Hesiod, but there is plenty of modern evidence that can be cited to support such a view. Although the psychoanalytic concept of the "subconscious" is hard to test scientifically, it is widely accepted; and we have seen the phenomenon of "blindsight" and other similar processes that show we are conscious of only part of what goes on in our brains. Some writers have described the brain as being in effect a series of automata – with the conscious self little more than a puppet controlled by unconscious forces.

ABOVE Some scientists hold the view that people are merely highly sophisticated robots, and that the idea of a conscious self with control over what happens is an illusion.

CREATIVITY

ABOVE Creativity, learning, and the ability to make choices are just some of the factors that argue against this view of humans as little more than machines.

More than a brain in a box?

Perhaps this should not come as too great a surprise. We all carry out pretty complicated activities – not just walking and other movements, but even driving a car – automatically, with little conscious effort. Once we have learned something, we often relegate it from our conscious mind for most of the time. However, it seems clear that we need to be conscious to learn. This in itself presupposes the wish and ability to ask questions (and, one suspects, this is closely connected to play). It is here that the limitations of the reductionist view of the brain – which sees consciousness and free will as unimportant illusions – becomes apparent. Any "theory of the brain" must include the ability to make the theory itself. After all, the neuroscientist who considers free will to be an illusion exercises choice in deciding whether to believe or refute such a theory. Why should a series of "brain modules" be so endlessly curious about itself and about the world? And why should such modules expend so much effort in trying to understand themselves?

We all accept that in our own personal lives we have the ability to ask questions and to make decisions and moral choices. These are often difficult, and we often make ill-advised decisions, but we cannot doubt the importance of consciousness and choice in our own lives. At the same time, few would deny that every thought in our brains corresponds to a physical "brain state." It is not easy to reconcile these two beliefs; but if we cannot reconcile them, it must mean that there is a problem in our understanding of ourselves or the world, or of both.

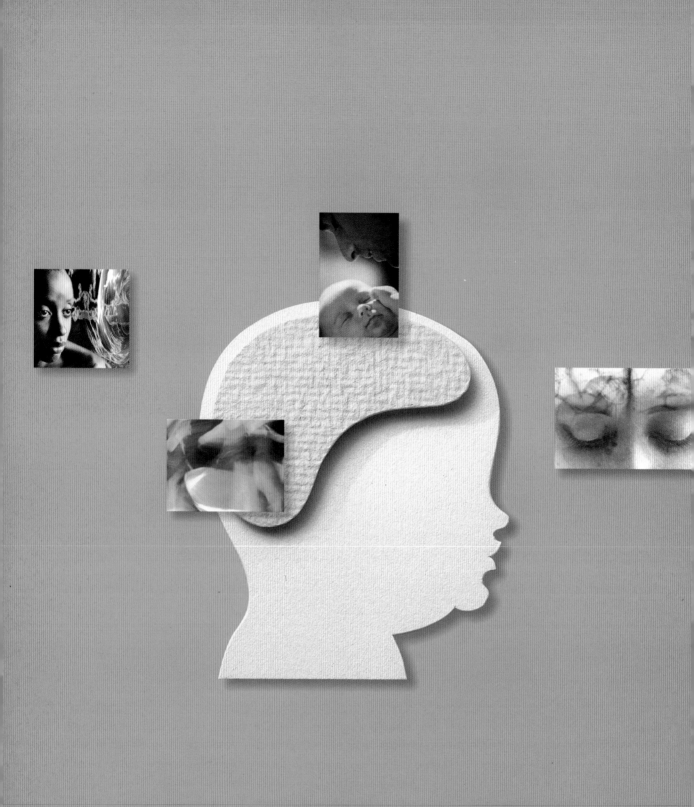

chapter two
the growing brain

From the moment of conception, the brain grows
at a fantastic rate, so that we arrive in the world
fully equipped with sensory abilities and the
beginnings of language.

The Growing Brain
introduction

ABOVE The complexity of the brain can be gauged from the fact that there are as many neurons in the brain as there are trees in the Amazon rain forest.

Within a month of fertilization, the human egg has grown in the womb into a creature with a recognizable brain. In full developmental spate, the embryonic brain will be expanding at the breathtaking rate of approximately 250,000 cells a minute. The final count will be some 100 billion neurons – as many neurons as there are currently trees in the Amazon rain forest – along with ten times as many supporting glial cells, which maintain a benign and nurturing environment for the neurons to work in. At the time of birth, all the brain cells the person will ever have are already there.

There can be enormous variation in the kind of work the neurons will do, depending on the direction and distance they migrate from the embryo's core brain region in order to make up the growing brain. We have already seen how within the brain increasingly complex circuits of neurons build up into sophisticated configurations, which can eventually be recognized as a specific brain area. These areas each have specialized contributions to make to the working of the brain; a big question in brain research, however, is precisely how they relate to the familiar yet awesome processes of which the brain is capable.

A century ago, the doctrine of "phrenology" misguidedly ascribed specific functions, in a simple one-to-one matching, to areas indicated by the bumps on an individual's skull, so as to produce a "brain map." Although this idea has long been discredited, there's still a widespread notion that one brain region must be responsible exclusively and autonomously for one single function – effectively that there is a series of mini-brains within the brain. We now know, however, that the brain is organized not as a chance hodgepodge of independent components, but

RIGHT The brain is organized symphonically, with each part relating to and connected with its neighbor to produce the whole.

more like a symphonic musical composition. Each brain region plays its own distinct role, yet it is a role that is always in concert with other regions – so that the whole is truly more than the sum of the parts. In this chapter we shall see how any particular function is divided up between many brain regions, and conversely how any one brain region plays a part in more than one brain function.

The speaking brain

One of the most intriguing of these functions is the only unique feature of the human brain, a feature not found at all in other animals: the ability to speak a language. So far as our understanding of the brain is concerned, language poses a mystery – in that we still do not know for sure how and why such a skill evolved in the human brain alone. Although non-human primates are capable of certain crude, rudimentary features of what we might call "language," the spontaneous ability to weave words into sentences seems to be the hallmark of the human brain. In this chapter we shall see how our brains are both similar and yet different from those of other animals in the way we interpret the world through our senses. The human brain is far from being a mere sponge, but plays an active part in determining what we perceive. We shall also discover how that perception is at the mercy of our previous experiences, and what happens when things go wrong.

LEFT Language, the mysterious ability to communicate our ideas, sensations, and emotions to others, is what sets the human race apart.

Language

ABOVE Language can be used to inform, persuade, encourage, inspire, threaten – it is infinitely adaptable.

Many species have sophisticated communication systems. Bees dance to indicate the direction of food. Songbirds use their calls to engage in courtship rituals. Monkeys have a wide repertoire of signals, which they use to help manage their elaborate social structures and warn of impending danger. Yet human beings sit at the pinnacle of sophisticated communication. No other species (as far as we know) has a communication system to match the exquisite accuracy of language. By flapping our tongues and making the air vibrate, we can conjure up very specific thoughts in the brains of others. And not just preadapted thoughts like "there's a snake approaching," but also unique, useless thoughts like "if you wink your left eye, I'll hop on my right leg."

How are we able to master such a sophisticated communication system? One obvious explanation is that language acquisition in humans takes a relatively long time (a good two to three years in the young of the species); maybe our complex linguistic abilities are the product of a protracted period of learning. But learning is not the sole prerogative of humans. Some birds reared in isolation are capable of learning songs that are not native to their species, providing that they only ever hear the non-native song. But given the choice of their native song and that of another species, they will acquire their own – some part of their brain is tuned to listen for a particular type of tune. Investigators of human language acquisition have suggested that our brains are also tuned to learn a particular type of communication system, but one that is far more complex than that of any songbird. The protracted period of human language acquisition reflects the need to learn. Nevertheless, this learning is based on a complex genetic endowment for language that is not possessed by any other species on the planet.

RIGHT Language is more than a matter of naming objects, although that may be how it begins. Language is creative as well as descriptive.

RIGHT There is strong evidence to suggest that our oldest ancestors did not possess the linguistic abilities that we have.

One of the puzzles of language is where it came from. For many of the other complex features of *Homo sapiens*, such as the eye, it is possible to trace the evolutionary tinkering that resulted in such a complex organism. For language, however, we cannot identify intermediate stages in its evolution. We don't know of any primitive languages or missing links that might help explain how this gift evolved. Studies of the vocal tract of Neanderthal humans suggest that they would have been incapable of producing the range of sounds that characterizes human speech. The implication is that language is a relatively recent achievement, probably less than 100,000 years old.

IS LANGUAGE INNATE?

THERE IS NO DOUBT that the ability of *Homo sapiens* to acquire language is innate. Our brains are tuned to pick up just the right kind of information from our environment so we can learn swiftly to communicate with our care givers and our peers. But what enables us to learn language so quickly, usually within three or four years? An important source of evidence in answering this question comes from language learning in brain-damaged children and adolescents. We have known for a long time that damage to the left hemisphere of the brain causes particular problems with language. However, the long-term effects of brain damage depend on when the damage occurs. For example, if you suffer damage to the language centers of the brain in adulthood or after puberty, you are much less likely to recover full language functioning than if the damage occurs before puberty, when cortical tissue is flexible enough for non-damaged areas to take over the function of the damaged areas. Infants who have the whole of the left hemisphere removed before they are six months old can go on to master language at a normal or near-normal level by the time they are four. Such results indicate that specific prewired pieces of cortical tissue are not needed for language learning to proceed successfully. Whatever is innate seems to have a more general or abstract quality.

RIGHT Humans possess a genetic matrix for acquiring language. It is as if there is a pattern that we fill in as we grow and pick up information from all around us.

Learning to talk

ABOVE From the moment they are born, children are developing a sensitivity to the significant sounds and patterns of their native language.

*N*ewborn infants seem completely helpless – but, in reality, we come into the world with an impressive set of abilities. We know how to recognize a human face, can tell the difference between speech and other sounds, and can even discriminate between our mother tongue and foreign languages.

However, despite these innate abilities, it takes us several years to achieve mastery of our mother tongue. Different languages make different demands, since the sounds, words, and grammar differ. Depending on which language you learn, you may need to pay attention to the order of the words in a sentence to figure out who is doing what to whom (as in English), or you may be able to figure it out from the endings of the words, irrespective of their position in the sentence (as in Turkish). Nevertheless, all over the world babies seem equally adept at learning language. A Japanese baby brought up in England will learn English as easily as an English baby would. Indeed, babies are much more flexible learners than their care givers. For example, Japanese adults find it difficult to tell the difference between "r" and "l" sounds, so "row" and "low" sound the same. But newborn Japanese infants are just as proficient as English ones at distinguishing "r" and "l," and this ability is retained until they are about a year old. In fact, newborn humans are sensitive to all the sound distinctions found across the world's languages, but by the age of 12 months they are sensitive only to the ones that are important in their own language. Around the same time, they start producing their first words.

The naming explosion

The word infant means "without language," and during the first year of life infants are not masters of their native tongue. They are developing a sensitivity to the sound patterns that characterize their own language, and their attempts at controlling the intricate mechanics of speech production is evident in their babbling; but this knowledge is not yet put to good use. All this

ABOVE Babies have much more flexible language acquisition skills than adults, such that a baby born in a foreign country will readily learn that country's language.

changes in the second year of life when children the world over begin to demonstrate their linguistic prowess. Early in the second year, they master just a few words – such as "more," "look," and "no" – usually to control the flow of goods and services from their care givers. However, later in the second year (often around 21 months), a dramatic spurt in development occurs. Children suddenly start producing lots of different words, usually names for objects and actions. From this "naming explosion" onward, vocabulary develops at the phenomenal rate of around ten words a day for the next four or five years.

LEFT By the time they are two, children have adequate control of language to be able to communicate simple messages such as "I'm hungry!"

Mastering the code

At the same time, children start to combine words to make up miniature sentences. And they don't just imitate what they hear. They are creative in their use of language, sometimes making intelligent errors, like pointing at a pair of sheep and saying "sheeps." This sudden mastery of language may well be the result of brain development during the second year. Indeed, the brain activity in a 15-month-old child on hearing a known word is different to the brain activity that occurs on hearing the same word six months later, by which time the naming explosion has occurred. Alternatively, it may be that the slow but sure progress that has taken place during the first year of life forms the foundations for the later accelerated growth. To put it another way, infants spend the first year or so cracking the language code; then once they have cracked it, there's no stopping them. Whatever the explanation, one thing is clear. By the middle of the third year of life, the linguistic capacity of the human child has far outstripped the communicative abilities of any other species on our planet.

BELOW A child of three or four has cracked the code, and from now on its linguistic development is a matter of acquiring more complex vocabulary and concepts – the structure is all in place.

THE LEARNING CURVE

Age	Ability	Age	Ability
Newborn	From birth, a baby is able to distinguish all speech sounds without discrimination in favor of their own language.	Second year	At the beginning of their second year, babies will begin to produce their first words. By the end of the second year, they have begun to extend their vocabulary at a fantastic rate.
First year	By twelve months babies are sensitive only to the speech sounds that are important for carrying meaning in their own language. They are babbling and following the speech rhythms of their care givers.	Third year onward	Children are now in command of their language structure, and development continues in terms of acquiring more sophisticated vocabulary from now on.

Left brain, right brain

The brain is divided into two hemispheres, left and right. In any individual the two hemispheres look almost identical, and neuroanatomical investigations reveal that every region on one side of the brain is connected to the equivalent network on the other side. Nevertheless, in the adult brain the two hemispheres are quite different in their functioning. Generally, the left hemisphere takes care of tasks involving symbolic processes (speech, reading, writing, and mathematics), while the right hemisphere deals with spatial relations and music.

Another way of describing this division of labor is in terms of the distinction between analytic and holistic thinking. This is perhaps best understood in terms of the way the brain processes music. We know that in the general population music results in preferential activation of the right hemisphere of the brain; in contrast, trained musicians show preferential activation of the left hemisphere. This difference is not due to innate differences between musicians and non-musicians – it is possible to observe the preferred hemisphere for music changing during the course of a musician's training. Musicians appear to listen to music in a different way from the general population: they listen in a more analytic fashion, rather than appreciating it holistically. Of course, this doesn't mean musicians lose their appreciation of music, they just appreciate it in a different way. In general, behavior that requires analytic intelligence engages the services of the left hemisphere, while the right hemisphere deals more with sensory perceptions and emotions.

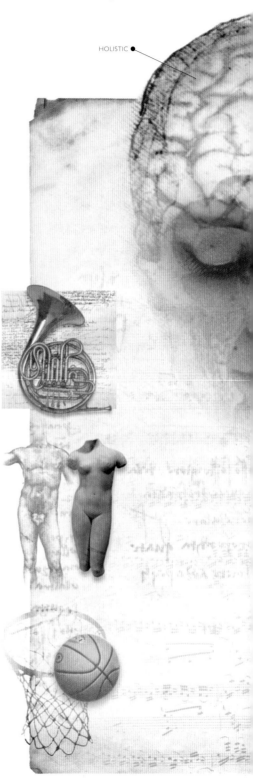

BELOW The reason for the division of functions between the two hemispheres of the adult brain is not fully understood. What is clear is that, by the time we reach puberty, the left side of the brain is analytical, while the right is more holistic.

HOLISTIC

ANALYTICAL

What is the reason for lateralization?

We still do not properly understand why the brain divides tasks in the way we observe in most people. After all, it would make perfectly good sense to have a region of the brain exclusively devoted to music but allow that part of the brain to change the way it works as a result of experience. As we have seen, infants who have had the whole of the left hemispheres removed before the age of six months can still grow up with normal language function, even though the left hemisphere is generally considered to be specialized for language. Evidently, the right hemisphere is flexible enough to take on unaccustomed functions if called upon to do so early enough in our development. Similarly, the left hemisphere can take over jobs that the right hemisphere would do in the event of severe early damage. If damage occurs later in life, however, the chances of complete recovery are much reduced.

How do the differences occur?

The differences in functioning between the two cerebral hemispheres may be due to a fundamental difference in the character of the neural systems in the two regions. It is possible that these differences may be present at birth and result in different behaviors being recruited by the two hemispheres. However, we have no neurophysiological data to confirm this theory, and it is more likely that initially the two hemispheres engage in a competition to carry out specific tasks.

For example, we know that in one-year-olds language understanding is distributed across both hemispheres, and that it becomes lateralized to the left hemisphere by the age of two. Subtle initial differences between the two hemispheres may result in the competition for particular tasks (say language or music) being won by a particular side; then once a hemisphere has won one battle, it may be easier for it to win the battle for other tasks that are similar. Hence, once an analytic task (such as language) has been assigned to a particular hemisphere (the left), other like-minded tasks follow suit. Before long, an analytic mode of processing can come to dominate an entire hemisphere. What initially started off as a subtle hemispheric difference can evolve through experience into global differentiation of function. We still have to discover what the initial subtle difference might be, especially since it is responsible for the stable pattern of hemispheric specialization observed in most individuals.

Language impairment

We have seen that language is the distinctive feature of human beings, and it is fundamental to the communication of our thoughts, ideas, desires, and feelings. The inability to control spoken or written language can therefore be very disabling, damaging sufferers' social and educational prospects, and in extreme cases preventing them from being able to communicate at all.

ABOVE Language impairment is caused by there being a piece missing from the complex jigsaw that is the brain's language production system. This could be a result of brain damage or some genetic disorder.

Language impairment comes in many forms. For example, people who suffer from Specific Language Impairment (SLI) appear to have perfectly normal intellectual abilities but experience difficulty with certain grammatical constructions – like getting the ending of verbs right, or understanding sentences with complicated syntax. Both developmental dyslexia (see opposite) and SLI appear to have genetic roots, as there is no obvious brain damage or neuroanatomical abnormality. However, there is much controversy over the source of these problems.

Some researchers attribute the impairment to a deficit in a central processing ability, such as inadequate knowledge of grammar or lack of awareness of the letter-to-sound rules. Others suggest that these impairments stem from deficits in peripheral processes associated with listening and reading.

Speech impairment

If the language centers of the brain (which in most people are located in the left cerebral hemisphere) are damaged, difficulty in using language results. Strictly, dysphasia is the term for partial loss of speech, and aphasia for total speech loss. However, the two names are often used interchangeably.

Injury to a specific area of the brain most commonly happens as a result of a stroke. A stroke occurs when a blood vessel supplying the brain either becomes obstructed – causing an infarct (death of tissue) from loss of blood supply – or bursts, causing a hemorrhage that results in the formation of a blood clot in the brain. If the blood vessel involved is a large one, a large area of the brain will be damaged; if it's a small vessel, only a small area will suffer. This is why the degree of dysphasia that occurs after a stroke varies considerably.

LEARNING TO READ is much more difficult than learning to speak, because it involves rapidly identifying letters, sequencing them, and matching them with the sounds they represent. The problem is that speech naturally divides into syllables, not into the smaller units known as phonemes that are represented by letters or a combination of letters. To read, we not only have to split written words into their separate letters visually, but also to divide spoken words into the separate phonemes that the letters represent.

Most people learn to read fairly fluently during childhood, but five to ten percent of all children (particularly boys) are developmental dyslexics: regardless of their level of intelligence, they cannot learn to read. "Developmental dyslexia" usually runs in families and is often associated with other abnormalities, such as left/right confusions and poor balance. Most scientists now accept that it has a genetic basis that causes mild impairment of the development of the brain. "Acquired dyslexia" can occur later in life as a result of brain damage affecting the left parietal association cortex, where the visual analysis of words and letters is associated with their sounds.

People with "surface" dyslexia lack the ability to divide words into their constituent sounds; consequently they cannot read or spell invented words, such as "tegwop." "Deep" dyslexics confuse words and their meaning, so might read "boat" as "ship." "Visual" dyslexics transpose and reverse letters, so tend to read "was" for "saw" or "dog" for "bog."

LEFT Reading is a very specialized skill, and dyslexia is not a reflection of lack of intelligence, but of a genetic deficiency that means this skill is difficult to acquire.

If the part of the speech area toward the front of the left hemisphere (called Broca's area) is damaged, many people develop expressive dysphasia. They can understand everything that is said to them and everything they read, but cannot find the words with which to express themselves. It is as if the words are on the tip of their tongues, but they are unable to remember them. In severe cases sufferers can utter nothing more than sounds; in milder cases they only have difficulty with certain words.

If the part of the speech area toward the back of the brain (Wernicke's area) is damaged, people tend to find it more difficult to understand what is said to them than to express themselves. This is known as receptive dysphasia. In practice, many people suffer a combination of expressive and receptive problems. If only small areas of the speech regions are damaged, disabilities may result that are more specific: for example, an inability to write (dysgraphia) despite a preserved ability to speak, or difficulties with particular grammatical forms.

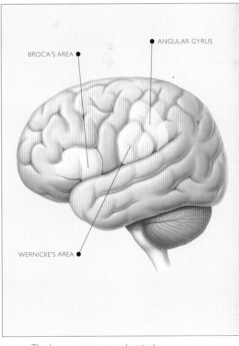

ANGULAR GYRUS

BROCA'S AREA

WERNICKE'S AREA

ABOVE The language areas are located, in most people, in the left hemisphere, around and above the ear. Each area is responsible for a different aspect of language production and reception.

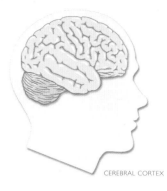

CEREBRAL CORTEX

The senses

Our sensory systems acquire information about the current state of the world by gathering signals from receptors in the eyes, ears, and other sense organs. The signals from one side of the body are sent through nerve fibers to the cerebral cortex on the opposite side of the brain, where they are perceived and interpreted in terms of our previous experiences, knowledge of the world, and expectations.

ABOVE Our perceptions of the world around us are generated by our brains on the basis of the information that our sense organs deliver during every second of our waking lives.

The signals need to encode only four fundamental properties of a stimulus:

1 what it is (its modality)
2 where it is in the outside world (its location)
3 when it starts, stops, or changes (its timing)
4 how much of it there is (its intensity)

All our complicated impressions of the outside world are built up from receptors encoding these four basic variables: what, where, when, and how much.

Modality and intensity
The exact nature of a sensation is signaled by the activation of modality-specific nerve fibers. Each fiber responds to only one modality – such as a particular color or type of sound – because the receptor to which it is linked has specific properties that convert only one form of sensory energy into nervous impulses.

The intensity of the stimulus, together with when it starts, stops, or changes, is signaled by the frequency of the nerve impulses generated by a single receptor. Changes in intensity are registered only if they exceed a given proportion of the background level. So you may be able to hear a helicopter's rotor, but not the buzzing of a fly trapped inside your car, above the roar of traffic on a freeway.

TIMING

THE TIMING of sensory events is the job of large neurons with rapid dynamics. Many receptors only respond at the beginning and end of stimulation; these on/off cells are said to show "rapid adaptation" or dynamic rather than static sensitivity. Their signals are conducted to the brain along large high-speed fibers, so any changes that might indicate danger or opportunity are brought rapidly to our attention.

Spatial relationships

To represent where a stimulus occurs, sensory pathways are mapped "topographically," so that adjacent points in the world are sensed by adjacent receptors in the skin or retina. The signals are then passed along nerve fibers to the brain, where the points are mapped in the primary receiving areas of the cerebral cortex. Because the center of your gaze, your lips, and your fingers and toes have the greatest density of receptors, the amount of cortex devoted to them is enormously expanded.

"Localizing" the features of an object in relation to one another depends on these topographical maps. Neighboring cells tend to inhibit each other; so when a visual cell on the bright side of an edge is excited, it inhibits its neighbor on the dark side, accentuating the edge. This arrangement means that the sensory cells tend to "fire" most for local changes created by new events, and nerve fibers are not wasted signaling things that don't change.

Information filters

Each sense is composed of many parallel channels, each devoted to extracting a particular type of information, such as form, color, or motion. Each of these channels consists of a series of processing stations that receive both input from below and suggestions from above about the nature of the object being analyzed. The areas of the cerebral cortex that carry out these processing operations are organized in columns. All the neurons in a column respond to the same region of space and the same kind of stimulus, so each column forms a processing module that passes on only the type of information it is specialized to detect.

Each sensory system also receives control signals from the cerebral cortex and brainstem, which can further filter incoming signals to select the most important. The analyzed and classified sensory patterns are then routed straight through to the motor systems that control behavior.

ABOVE The neurons that alert us to changes in the world around us send messages at high speed. In evolutionary terms, this is to allow us the maximum time to act or to escape.

Vision

VISUAL CORTEX

LIGHT

DISTANCE

SPEED

The performance of the human visual system is phenomenal. When fully dark-adapted, you can see faint lights that emit only 10 photons, but bright sunlight floods your eyes with 1,000 million times that number. In daylight you can resolve two points that are less than one tenth of a millimeter apart from a distance of three feet away, and you can discern a difference of less than a millimeter in the depth of a surface. You can detect movement as slow as a tenth of a millimeter per second, yet as fast as 10 yards per second; and you can distinguish more than 300 different colors.

The cornea and lens of the eye focus light rays onto the retina, which contains the light receptors, called rods and cones. Cones recognize color, while the larger rods are more sensitive to light (we rely on rods when there is very little light). The cornea does most of the focusing for distance vision; the lens adds its bit by varying its curvature for objects closer to the eye. When a cell absorbs light, a message is sent that shuts off an electrical current that is continuous in the dark. This signals the light. Its color is signaled by whichever type of cone is most affected.

Another layer of the retina contains the "ganglion cells," which have nerve fibers connecting to the thalamus and the primary visual cortex. There are two main types: the large, fast "magno" cells conduct information about timing to the visual cortex, while the smaller, slower "parvo" types process color.

ABOVE AND RIGHT The sensitivity of the human visual system allows us to perform a wide range of operations, such as spotting extremely slow movements or detecting tiny objects.

Optical crossover

The signals from the retina pass along the optic nerve. The nerve fibers cross over at a position called the optic chiasm, perhaps to help correct the optical reversing effect of the lens of the eye, and then fan out to the primary visual area of the occipital

RIGHT The recognition of different aspects of what is seen, such as color and motion, is governed by specific areas of the visual cortex, the part of the brain that receives signals from the eye.

THE STRUCTURE OF THE EYE

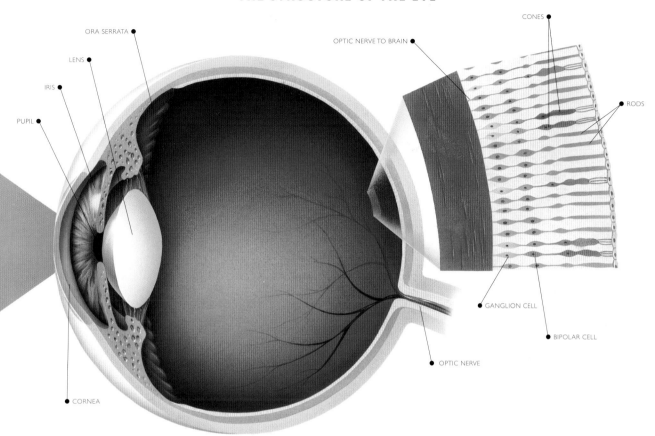

ORA SERRATA

LENS

IRIS

PUPIL

CORNEA

OPTIC NERVE TO BRAIN

OPTIC NERVE

CONES

RODS

GANGLION CELL

BIPOLAR CELL

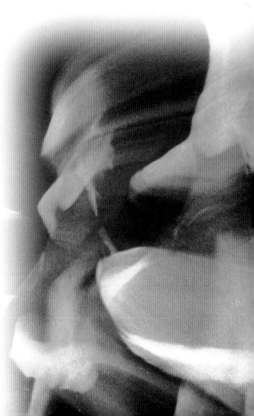

cortex, the area known as V1. The crossover arrangement means that signals dealing with one half of visual space are relayed to the visual cortex on the opposite side.

The visual receptive fields in V1 are organized in columns. The set of columns excited by a particular visual target defines its outline and contours, and begins the task of identifying it. Other columns recognize direction of motion, color, and "binocular disparity" – the difference between the position of each eye's image of an object. Since this disparity depends on the distance of the object, it adds the third dimension – depth – to the flat two-dimensional view of the world provided by each retina.

Selective blindness

Because the visual cortex contains over 30 different areas, each devoted to analyzing different features, lesions on the cortex can cause blindness to certain specific features only. Lesions on the lower part of the temporal cortex affect sensitivity to the fine detail of shape and color, causing an inability to recognize objects, while damage to the posterior part of the parietal cortex affects sensitivity to location and movement.

Hearing

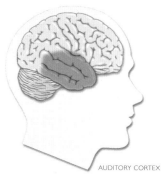

AUDITORY CORTEX

S ound waves are rather like the waves of compression that travel down a long spring when it is struck at one end; they consist of longitudinal waves of intermittent compression in the air. Most acoustic information, such as speech or music, is carried by changes in the amplitude (loudness) and frequency (pitch) of sound waves.

Inside the ear

As sound waves enter the ear canal, they vibrate the eardrum, which is linked to the fluid-filled cochlea in the inner ear by three tiny bones. These bones are supplied with muscles that protect against very loud sounds and filter out confusing frequencies. Since the eardrum has 20 times the area of the entrance to the cochlea, the waves are amplified so they move the fluid in the cochlea. In turn, the fluid moves hair cells that convert the waves into nervous impulses.

There are two types of hair cell. The outer hair cells contract in time with the sound waves and amplify them even more. The inner hair cells respond to pitch, being tuned so those at the base of the spiral cochlea respond best to high frequencies and those higher up signal lower frequencies. The sensitivity of both sets of hair cells can also be regulated by the brain via the "olivo-cochlear bundle."

Stereophonic awareness

The auditory nerve axons run to the cochlear nuclei in the brain-stem. Each nucleus is sharply tuned to the resonant frequency of the hair cells supplying it, and the auditory relays are mapped "tonotopically" – so that, as in the cochlea, neighboring neurons represent neighboring tone frequencies.

The system locates sound sources by comparing the input to the two ears. Two-thirds of the cochlear nuclei axons project across the brainstem to the area called the "superior olivary nucleus" on the other side, while the rest pass to the superior olivary nucleus on the same side. Since the head acts as a baffle,

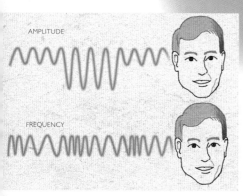

AMPLITUDE

FREQUENCY

ABOVE Sound has two basic characteristics: loudness, which depends on the size of the sound waves, and pitch, which depends on their frequency.

at high frequencies the cells in each nucleus are most strongly excited by sounds coming from the opposite side, and the difference between the stimulation of the cells in the nuclei indicates where the sound is coming from. At lower frequencies, the system detects the difference in the time it takes for sounds to reach the nearer ear compared with the further ear.

From the superior olivary nucleus, the acoustic signals are carried to the primary auditory cortex in the temporal lobe. This also contributes to localizing sound sources and analyzes the amplitude and frequency modulations that distinguish speech sounds and other acoustic signals.

ABOVE Listening to music is a fantastically complex mental process, since it involves both translating the various sound waves into a meaningful pattern, and recognizing and responding to the emotional content of the piece.

BELOW The inner ear is a complicated arrangement of tiny bones, muscles, and hair cells that translate sound waves into nervous impulses that are sent to the brain for analysis.

SPEECH AND HEARING

THE ABILITY TO HEAR is obviously closely connected with the capacity to produce and understand language. At one extreme, deafness prevents the sufferer from registering speech or any other sounds, thus making language acquisition very difficult. However, disorders of the auditory association areas will also have an effect on a person's linguistic ability. It has been suggested that Specific Language Impairment (see page 54) may be a result of a deficit in the ability to process speech sounds, particularly consonantal sounds, quickly. When someone speaks to you at normal conversational speed, you have to be able to recognize the difference between, say, the sound "t" and the sound "d" very rapidly in order to distinguish the different words. If you cannot identify the speech sounds, learning grammar and other aspects of language becomes extremely difficult.

THE OPERATION OF THE EAR

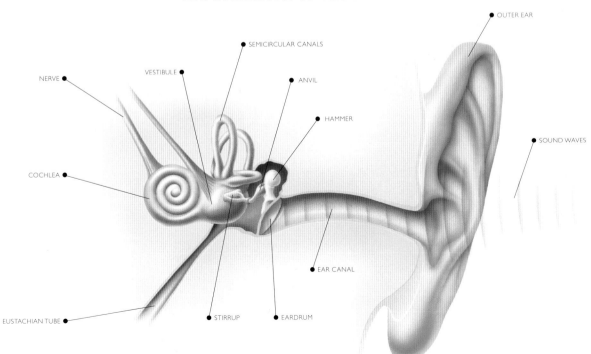

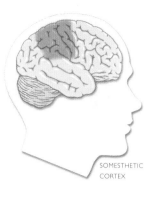

SOMESTHETIC
CORTEX

Touch and pain

*T*he skin is equipped with sensors that register a variety of bodily sensations. These include light touch, pressure, flutter, and vibration, as well as heat, cold, and pain. Other sensors register joint position and muscle sensations.

The inputs are registered by different receptors, each tuned to a particular type of sensation. Among them are the Meissner's and Pacinian corpuscles in the skin, each consisting of onionlike layers of cells surrounding a large nerve fiber, which conducts the inputs rapidly to the central nervous system. These corpuscles signal only the initial stimuli, such as the first touch on the skin, then adapt and so stop discharging.

Merkel's disks and Ruffini endings are expanded tips of nerve fibers that lie within the folds of the fingerprints. When moisture from the sweat glands temporarily sticks the skin whorl to a surface, they deform. This makes them exquisitely sensitive to movements of the skin over a surface. Sensations of warmth, cold, and pain are signaled by the bare nerve endings of thin slow-conducting fibers.

The strength of a stimulus is encoded by the number of impulses generated in excess of the background level, and this proportional relationship is transmitted to the somesthetic cortex, the part of the brain that deals with touch. The density of receptors on the lips and fingers is much higher than on the back of the legs or trunk, which is why the fingers and lips have such good spatial resolution.

Sensory fibers
The largest afferent nerves from the skin form a bundle of fibers that passes up the back of the spinal cord. Known as dorsal columns, they make their first relay in a nucleus in the lowest part of the brainstem, so the fibers from the toes of a tall man can be as much as six feet (two meters) long.

BELOW AND RIGHT These models show a normal body and what the body would look like if the size of its different parts was in proportion to the density of the touch receptors in those areas. This demonstrates clearly how some parts of the body are much more sensitive to touch than others.

LIPS

HANDS

GENITALS

FEET

RIGHT As with many other kinds of sense perception, the feelings registered by the sense organs on one side of the body are dealt with by the brain hemisphere on the opposite side.

The neurons in the dorsal-column nucleus respond to pressure. They have strong surround inhibition, to enhance any edges that are felt, and they filter out unimportant touch signals, such as the pressure of the seat you're sitting on. The axons of the neurons on one side change places with those on the other before running via the thalamus to the primary somesthetic cortex (S1). This means that S1 on one side deals with signals from the opposite side of the body.

Some of the smaller fibers from the skin sensors do not pass straight to the brainstem, but relay where they enter the spinal gray matter, so that their information is initially analyzed. Secondary axons then take messages up the front columns of fibers in the spinal cord to the brainstem and the primary somesthetic cortex.

The representations in S1 magnify signals from the lips, tongue, fingers, and toes, because they have such a high density of receptors. Like other areas of the cortex, S1 is organized in columns of neurons dealing with the same area of skin and the same type of sensation. The much smaller secondary somesthetic cortex (S2), situated beside S1, represents both halves of the body, receives more of the pain inputs, and is highly sensitive to movement.

LIPS

HANDS

FEET

Damage to the somesthetic cortex

Injury or damage to S1 destroys the sensation of touch and causes astereognosis, an inability to identify objects by feeling them. But pain sensations persist, although they are harder to localize, because the main representation of pain happens in another area of the brain, the anterior cingulate gyrus. The control of movement by feedback from skin and muscles is also often relatively unaffected, because the motor cortex receives inputs direct from the muscles or via the cerebellum.

The somesthetic areas of the front part of the parietal cortex project back to the rear part. Any damage here interferes with movement greatly, and the patient's perception of his or her body is distorted. One symptom of this is "dressing apraxia," where the patient fails to dress one side of the body because she or he has no awareness of its existence.

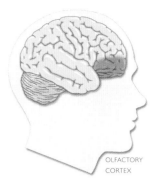

OLFACTORY
CORTEX

Smell and taste

ABOVE Perfumes tap directly into our brain's emotional center.

*I*n evolutionary terms, smell is the most ancient of the sensations, and the limbic system – the unconscious part of the brain that deals with motivation and emotions – developed from it. Accordingly, human behavior is more driven by our responses to smell than we might care to admit. Our choice of sexual partner, for instance, is very much influenced by personal odors, called pheromones, that we are hardly even conscious of.

TASTE RECEPTORS

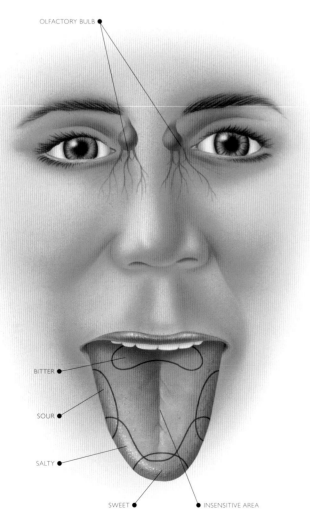

OLFACTORY BULB

BITTER

SOUR

SALTY

SWEET   INSENSITIVE AREA

The importance of our sense of smell can be observed throughout history. The main impetus for the voyages of Marco Polo and Columbus was to discover a shorter sea route to the Orient to make it easier to import the strong spices needed to mask the taste and smell of poorly preserved meat. Indeed, these were so much in demand in Europe before the development of refrigeration that in the Middle Ages they were worth more than their weight in gold. Even today, people are willing to pay a small fortune for perfumes to make them more attractive to the opposite sex (although the most important ingredient of perfumes is the musky secretion from the highly unromantic anal gland of the civet).

Olfactory refinement

The tissue in the nose contains 40 million hair cells. A gene complex generates an astronomical number of receptor proteins, each of which responds to a particular odorant. When a receptor is triggered, the hair cell releases a transmitter that then sends a signal along the olfactory fibers. These pass through the roof of the nose to the olfactory bulb, right in the front of the brain.

LEFT There are only four basic taste areas on the tongue, and thus taste is quite a primitive sense in comparison with the others.

From there, nerves deliver smell signals to the primary olfactory cortex, which feeds directly into the limbic drive system.

Different smells can be distinguished because each generates a specific pattern of electrical activity (called an electroolfactogram) in the olfactory bulb, and these patterns trigger similar responses in the primary olfactory cortex. These signals are then passed on to the frontal lobe, where they are linked with taste signals. If the signal is pleasant, it acts as a "reward," encouraging whatever behavior produced it – for instance, smelling a rose or eating an ice cream.

Our whole motivational network has evolved from the olfactory system, which is why smells play such a subversively important part in our lives, particularly our sex lives. This connection is demonstrated by Kallman's syndrome, in which the neurons responsible for controlling the secretion of sex hormones fail to migrate from their origin in the nose to the hypothalamus, a process that usually takes place in the womb four months after conception. As a result, sexual development cannot take place, and in addition the sufferer has no sense of smell.

BELOW The pleasure of eating derives as much, if not more, from the smell and the appearance of the food as from its taste, since our range of taste sensations is very limited.

RESTRICTED TASTE

TASTE IS A MUCH more limited sense, and much of the pleasure of food and drink is really a response to its smell. There are only four basic tastes: sweet (sugars), sour (acids), salty (inorganic anions), and bitter (alkaloids). These are detected by taste buds, which are grouped in certain areas of the tongue (the sweetness receptors, for example, are concentrated mainly at the tip of the tongue). For some reason, taste buds have a lifespan of only about seven days, regenerating every week under the control of the gustatory nerve fibers.

Signals from the taste buds pass to the same nucleus in the brainstem as the "chemoreceptors" in the arteries that "taste" the acidity of the blood, and the ones in the stomach that taste the sweetness of food. From the brainstem the messages are passed, via the thalamus, to the primary taste area in the frontal lobe of the cortex, where they combine with the smell messages coming from whatever it is you are eating.

Supersenses

In broad terms, our human senses are well suited to our general needs, but individually their performance is eclipsed by the specialized senses found in many animals. This is because the senses evolve to meet the needs of the animal that uses them. Many animals have developed specific lifestyles that maximize their chances of survival – hence some hunt only at night, or live only in deserts, or have a specialized food supply. Humans are much less specialized, but more adaptable.

EAGLE ❶

HONEYBEE ❷

Animals frequently rely on one particular sense that has therefore become very highly developed. For example, although our eyes contain cone cells that are small enough to resolve points 1 inch apart from a distance of 100 yards, from the same range an eagle is able to distinguish points that are only ¼ inch apart. The eagle's cones are no smaller than ours, but those on the optical axis of an eagle's eye lie in a deep pit, with the more superficial receptors overlapping the deeper ones. As a result, they can achieve resolutions equivalent to one third of the cone diameter. In practical terms, this means that from a height of 300 feet, an eagle can distinguish a mouse from a vole and take its pick.

PIT VIPER ❸

Ultraviolet and infrared

We also have fairly limited color vision compared with other creatures. Honeybees and moths, for instance, are sensitive to ultraviolet light, so they see patterns on flowers that we cannot see. Many flowers exploit this, having bright ultraviolet patches on their petals that indicate where the nectaries are, making sure that potential pollinators pass close to the anthers, which dust them with pollen.

At the other end of the light spectrum, our temperature sense is very crude compared to that of some snakes. A rattlesnake or

❶ Eagles can detect tiny movements from hundreds of feet up in the sky, which is why they are such efficient hunters.

❷ Honeybees are sensitive to ultraviolet light patches on certain kinds of flowers.

❸ Snakes have highly sensitive heat-seeking sensors for hunting their prey at night.

OWL ⑥

ELECTRIC EEL ⑤

ARCTIC TERN ④

pit viper, although it has a very primitive visual system compared to ours, has a set of highly sensitive heat receptors clustered in the paired pit organs below its eyes. These receptors sense the infrared radiation given off by its warm-blooded prey, allowing the snake to target its victim accurately in total darkness. The expensive infrared "snooperscopes" and night cameras used by the police and military and in making wildlife films work in a similar way.

Rustles and clicks

Although our ears are exquisitely responsive to the nuances of sound in music, they are no match in terms of sensitivity for those of an owl or bat. Owls hunt in darkness, and their ears are so sensitive that from a height of several yards they can hear the rustle of a mouse's tiny feet. Owls also have one ear placed higher on their head than the other, which helps them to determine how far above their prey they are.

Insect-eating bats emit ultrasound clicks that are outside the range of our hearing. A bat can hear them, though, and it can also hear their echoes reflected from obstacles and by prey moving about in the dark. The bat's analysis of reflected sound waves is so precise that it can determine the position, size, speed, and direction of a moth with enough accuracy to catch it. But some moths can hear the bat's clicks, too, and have evolved ways of mimicking them, so as to confuse the signals and send the bat off in the wrong direction.

④ Migrating birds are equipped to detect the Earth's magnetic field so as to be able to navigate.

⑤ Some fish track their prey by detecting changes in the electromagnetic field of the water around them, indicating the presence of another fish.

⑥ The ears of an owl can detect faint sounds that would be inaudible to human ears.

ELECTROMAGNETIC SENSES

AS WELL AS HAVING highly developed versions of human senses, some animals possess sensory abilities that we do not share at all. For example, the electric organs of some fish emit voltage pulses from the fish's equivalent of the ear; to locate its prey, the fish analyzes any disturbances in the resulting electrical field. Sharks can detect the faint electrical signals produced by the firing neurons of their understandably nervous victims, and so are able to home in on them in the submarine gloom. Most spectacularly, electric eels can produce an electric pulse that is strong enough to stun or kill their prey.

Many animals have extraordinary navigational abilities. Salmon return to the river where they were born to reproduce, guided apparently by their sense of smell. Birds have a magnetic sense that helps them find their way during migration flights. The arctic tern, for example, migrates from the Arctic to the Antarctic and back again every year, a round trip of 11,000 miles. It has small crystals of soft iron in its body that act like a compass; they maintain their position in alignment with the Earth's magnetic field, giving the bird an inbuilt sense of direction.

Culture and the senses

ABOVE Language reflects the society that creates it and the types of events, emotions, activities, and objects that are important in that society.

*A*lthough we are all equipped with the same basic sensory apparatus, the way we make use of our senses varies widely. In general, a culture will highlight interpretations of artefacts in their own idiosyncratic way. Culture acts as a filter on our senses, highlighting certain objects and events while passing over others.

This does not mean that we actually see things differently: physically, the Inuit people of the Arctic and Londoners see snow in exactly the same way. However, our functional interpretation of objects and events, and hence their importance to us, can differ radically from one culture to the next. The Inuit need to be able to identify different types of snow in order to decide what equipment is needed for hunting. Our senses provide the landscape for our lives; our culture provides the infrastructure by which we negotiate that landscape.

BELOW Culture makes us see things differently, not in a literal sense – the colors and perspective are still the same – but in terms of the importance that we attach to particular features.

ABOVE Music is a specialized form of language with its own written conventions, and learning this language depends as much on cultural factors as does acquiring verbal language skills.

ALTHOUGH WE ACQUIRE LANGUAGE apparently effortlessly as infants, language learning as an adult is a very different process and works quite differently. Our early linguistic environment helps to determine our subsequent ability to perceive the subtler sounds in our language – and recent research suggests that our linguistic environment may have more far-reaching effects, as well. People raised in different areas (for example, California and the south of England) interpret some ambiguous changes in musical notes quite differently. This suggests that our perception of music, and hence our musical tastes, may partly be determined by the environment in which we grow up. You can try out some of these musical illusions using a CD available via the Internet from http://www.philomel.com

Language and culture

Language is one of the most important tools that a culture uses to sharpen and direct our senses. Simply by naming objects and events with nouns and verbs, we draw attention to their importance for us. Of course, the names for objects and actions vary from one language to the next – but so do the objects and actions that a language and culture choose to name. For example, some languages (such as Dani, from Papua New Guinea) have only two color words in their vocabularies, while others (among them English) have eleven. Some languages require that you indicate the shape of an object whenever you describe an action involving it (Navaho). Other languages include a grammatical inflection of the verb that indicates whether an event described by the speaker has been witnessed in person rather than merely reported (Turkish).

Languages vary enormously in terms of the facts they highlight about the world. Notice that these facts are almost always communicable across languages – otherwise I would not be able to tell you they exist. But because languages insist that their speakers pay attention to certain details, and because those details are often encoded in the language in a concise way, they become more accessible to speakers of that particular language. This process is similar to that experienced by anyone who develops an expertise in a skill or in the domain of scholarship: you need to learn a specialized vocabulary to go with a particular skill. Being an expert involves recognizing what is essential and what can be ignored. Language provides the members of a culture with a framework for deciphering what is important for their society. It also offers the young a form of social apprenticeship.

ABOVE Although it is often said that music is a universal language, our reactions to different kinds of music will depend to some extent on the musical environment in which we grew up.

Disorders of sensation

*T*here are many ways in which sensation can be altered or lost as a result of disease or physical injury affecting the brain. Sensation starts with the peripheral nervous system (for example, the nerves in the skin) sending messages to the central nervous system (the brain and spinal cord). The type of sensory disturbance suffered depends on where the damage has occurred in the chain between the ends of the peripheral nerves and the "higher" levels of the brain.

RIGHT Damage to a nerve, such as that caused by a blow, produces a painful sensation in the damaged area.

RIGHT There can sometimes be "phantom" pain messages from nerves that have been severed after amputation.

Damage to a peripheral nerve will produce pain if the damage is partial – such as the effect caused by hitting your "funny bone" (the ulnar nerve at the elbow) – or loss of feeling if the damage is complete. We are all familiar with the effect of disrupting a nerve ending from the numbness produced by a local anesthetic at the dentist's office. However, completely cutting a nerve does not always lead to permanent loss of feeling. People who have had a limb amputated can develop phantom limb pain – an unpleasant sensation of pain in the missing limb. Although this phenomenon is not clearly understood, it is as though the severed nerve endings in the limb stump send messages to the brain to create the illusion that the severed limb still exists.

Spinal injuries

Damage to the spinal cord may also result in illusions of severe pain. These may be experienced by people who have received a spinal injury in a car crash, or who suffer from diseases such as multiple sclerosis or syryngomyelia (a progressive disease of the spinal cord). People often find it difficult to describe such pain, but use words like "raw" or "burning." Some people who have suffered damage to the spinal cord will have no normal sensation or movement in their body below the level of the injury and yet, as with phantom-limb sensations, suffer severe pain.

If areas of the brain involved in sensation are damaged, more complex kinds of sensory disturbance can result. Most people think of epilepsy as involving physical convulsions and loss of consciousness, but it can affect almost any cerebral cortical function. Sensory epilepsy, for example, causes people to experience brief episodes of altered sensation, usually down one side of the body; and some forms of epilepsy characteristically start with the hallucination of a strange, and usually unpleasant, smell.

MISSING LIMBS

THE SENSORY AREAS of the parietal lobes are where the more complex analysis and integration of sensation occur. Damage to these areas, for instance through a tumor or a stroke, can result in people "losing" one half of their body – the half opposite to the injured side of the brain. This phenomenon of "loss" may apply to the external world, too. In severe cases, patients sometimes fail to recognize one of their own limbs and complain that somebody else's leg or arm is in bed with them. They may also be unable to perceive one half of a plate of food, and will only eat the food on the other half of the plate.

LEFT Spinal damage can result in severe pain, even though normal sensation below the injury has been lost.

LEFT It is possible to lose all feeling on one side of the body if the sensory area of the brain on the opposite side is damaged.

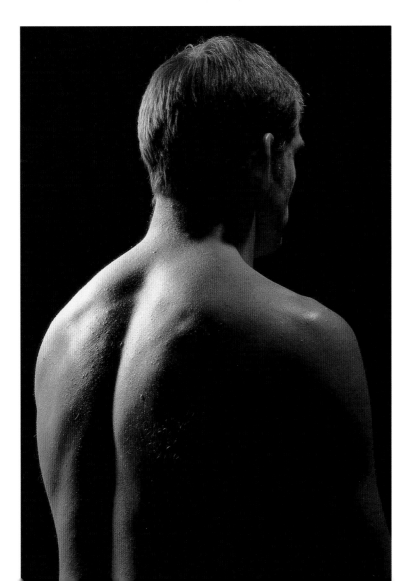

LEFT The spinal cord is the central pathway for transmitting sensations such as touch, heat, texture, and pain from the body's receptors to the brain.

chapter three
the young brain

The brain's childhood is the period when its basic functions develop. The next stage is the refinement of the qualities that distinguish us as individuals, in particular our emotional characters.

The Young Brain
introduction

By the time we reach adolescence, the brain is more or less mature in its basic functions: we can speak and understand speech, our senses are working as well as they ever will, and our movements are agile and well coordinated. Now begins a period during which occurs the development and refinement of much of what makes us not just uniquely human but also unique as individuals. Although many neuroscientists concentrate on our impressive ability to learn and remember, an equally important area of inquiry is into how our emotions develop and function.

ABOVE An infant's brain makes an enormous number of neural connections in a very short time, so all our basic functions are in place at an early age.

Emotions are not usually associated with studies of the brain. The analogy that is frequently made between the brain and a computer does not leave room for the idea of emotions, and yet emotions are essential to our proper functioning. In this chapter we shall be exploring how emotions contribute to the most basic aspects of our lives, what happens when they are disrupted, and how they can be changed and manipulated by drugs.

At the basis of all these issues lies a single factor: body chemistry. When we look at the anatomy of the brain and see how it breaks down into circuits of cells, or study the senses and examine how sounds, light, and smells are converted into the brain language of electrical impulses, it is easy to forget that chemicals play

LEFT The emotional growth that occurs as an older child moves toward adulthood is as significant as the rapid cognitive development that occurs during the first years.

an equally important part. However, as we shall see in this chapter, a certain class of chemical substances plays a vital role in integrating brain and body. These chemicals – hormones – have different actions compared to the fast, precise transmitter process that enables one neuron to communicate with another across a synapse. Hormones are far slower to act and pervade not just the brain but the bloodstream as well. We shall see how their action underscores our basic body functions and urges, and how these control systems are influenced by the activity of the brain itself. For example, the rhythms of sleep are con-

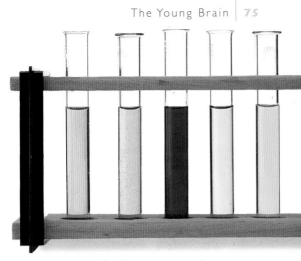

ABOVE Chemical transmitters, called hormones, help to control and regulate a range of bodily functions and activities, from reproduction and growth to temperature control.

trolled not only by our biorhythms, but also by different transmitters in the brain being operative at different times. Our sexual and reproductive systems are also maintained by hormonal activity that is regulated automatically by the brain.

System malfunction

This chapter also looks at what happens when these control systems malfunction. For example, we are equipped with a coordinated set of responses that enable the body to move quickly in a situation requiring immediate action. But nowadays these caveman responses are often elicited not by physical danger but under threat from more sophisticated perils – not because you

are going to be eaten by a tiger, but because there is a danger of losing your job. The aberrant and persistent activation of such responses are what we know as stress. And stress is not the only problem caused by modern living. Depression and the drugs that people use to escape from it, whether prescribed or proscribed, is a vital concern not just to neuroscientists, but to society as a whole.

LEFT Stress is not a modern invention, but a distortion of the body's natural response to danger; running or fighting is not an option when faced with the threats posed by twenty-first-century society.

Emotions

Emotions play a central part in our lives. Intense emotion can motivate and reward us, but equally it can punish us. Emotional expressions provide us with an extremely versatile channel of communication. The role of emotions in our lives leads to a number of questions. Is emotion a uniquely human phenomenon? Or is it something that we share with other animals? Are our emotions innate, or do we have to develop our emotional capacities and learn our emotional repertoire? What kinds of things arouse emotional responses in us?

Facial expressions are vital for emotional communication. We easily recognize signs of fear or anger, and our ability to recognize them doesn't depend on our cultural background. When photographs of actors displaying strong emotions were shown to members of isolated tribes in Papua New Guinea, their identification of the emotions portrayed coincided with that of Westerners. Although clearly we sometimes learn what to be frightened of, we don't need to learn how to express fear or how to recognize it in others. We are also sensitive to more subtle facial signs of emotion. When we are frightened or anxious, the pupils of our eyes contract; when we are happy or sexually aroused, they expand. If people are asked to rate the physical attractiveness of photographs of faces that have been manipulated to make the pupils larger or smaller, they rate the versions with expanded pupils as more attractive, even though they can't necessarily say why they chose the ones they did. Facial expressions are not just important for adult interactions, however; they also play a key role in communications between mothers and their babies.

LEFT Emotion has a key role in establishing a relationship between children and parents; in evolutionary terms, it is important that the parent has every incentive to take care of the child, and preserve its genes.

Reading faces

Other primates also read emotions through facial expressions. Monkeys can clearly recognize threats or signs of friendliness in others. These abilities depend on a brain structure called the amygdala (from the Greek word for almond, because of its shape). Damage to the amygdala profoundly compromises a monkey's ability to operate successfully in social groups, because it cannot interpret other monkeys' responses or predict their intentions. Human patients who have suffered amygdala damage are unable to identify facial expressions, even though they may know perfectly well who the faces belong to; nor can they identify emotions, such as anger, in recorded voices. Curiously enough, the opposite pattern is discernible in patients suffering from a disorder called prosopagnosia. They cannot recognize faces, even the faces of those who are closest to them, but they are able to interpret facial expressions normally. It would therefore appear that the ability to recognize the meaning of facial expressions is quite separate from the ability to recognize who the face belongs to.

Learned emotions

Although some emotional responses are probably pre-programmed, others are undoubtedly learned. The mechanisms for this may also depend on activity in the amygdala. Humans and other animals can learn to make associations between events that give intense pleasure or pain and signals, such as smells or sounds, that on their own may not mean anything at all. If the signal predicts that something significant is about to happen, then we respond to the signal as if it was as significant as the event it predicts. So a signal of impending pain will make us feel anxious. This provides a way in which our behavior can adapt to what is going to happen to us, rather than just responding to what has already happened. Hence, acquired emotions can be powerful aids to survival.

WANTS AND NEEDS

Psychologists often draw a distinction between drives and emotions. Drives like hunger or thirst have an obvious role in bodily regulation. Hunger depends on our energy levels and how long it is since last we ate: these drives are generated by our internal state. Emotions like fear arise in a different way: they are a response to the world around us. So maybe drives depend on our internal world, while emotions depend on our external world.

But this distinction is oversimple. It's true that we feel hungry when we are deprived of food, but our appetites are also aroused when we have been given just a taste of something delicious (the salted peanut effect: eating a couple of peanuts often makes us want to eat more). This is called an incentive effect. Sex drives have a high incentive component. Our internal state (e.g. how long it is since we last had sex) matters, but the world outside us matters a great deal, too (sexual desire can be excited by what we see, or touch).

BELOW Eating a few peanuts makes us want more; appetite is not just an internal drive.

Fear and phobia

We are right to be wary of many things in the world around us. If our distant ancestors had not been frightened of poisonous snakes and large hungry carnivores, we might not be here now. Fear can protect us from danger; but if fears aroused by harmless things become so strong as to cause significant distress, they cease being life-savers and turn into dangers themselves.

Such overwhelming fears are called phobias. Some, termed simple phobias, are fears of specific things; these afflict some ten percent of the population. Other types of phobia include fear of social situations and agoraphobia (fear of open space or of going outdoors), which is often associated with a tendency to suffer panic attacks. Some agoraphobics have effectively been confined by their phobia to their homes for years. Fears like these are not protective; they are destructive.

Some phobias are much more common than others. This wouldn't be surprising if the most common phobias were all concerned with really dangerous things; but they aren't. Arachnophobia (fear of spiders) is relatively common, even though spiders do not pose much of a threat to humans; cars are far more dangerous. Why, then, aren't there lots of car phobics and very few spider phobics? And what makes something specially likely to induce a phobia? It may be that we are biologically prepared to fear certain things. Perhaps our distant ancestors were more vulnerable to spiders than we are; small mammals are certainly vulnerable to large spiders, such as tarantulas. If evolutionary pressures led our forebears to develop an innate fear of spiders, that might explain why, even now, we are more likely to be frightened of them than of more modern – and more real – dangers, such as cars. It is possible that our evolutionary history has not caught up with our present circumstances. But how can we test a theory of this kind? One way might be to see whether species that share some distant ancestors with us also share our sensitivities to phobic stimuli.

Monkeys do easily develop a profound fear of snakes. But are baby monkeys fearful when they first encounter a snake, or do they learn to be frightened? It now seems that one critical determinant is the behavior of other monkeys. If other monkeys show signs of being scared of snakes, then it is more likely that a young monkey will develop a similar fear. So for monkeys, fear of biologically significant threats seems to be acquired partly by imitation, or social learning.

Treating phobias

Treatment for phobias changed radically with the introduction of behavior therapies. If a patient is so scared of spiders that he or she manages to avoid them altogether, then there's no way to learn by experience that spiders are actually harmless, so the phobia could persist forever. How can therapists get around this problem? They start by exposing the patient to something that's much less threatening than a large active spider – perhaps the patient is required only to imagine a spider, while the therapist provides reassurance or helps the patient to relax. The treatment then moves on to more and more intense examples, until eventually the patient can handle tarantulas without experiencing fear. These treatments are usually highly effective.

This gradual desensitization seems so obvious and sensible that it's surprising it took so long for it to be introduced. In fact, these treatments were inspired by early-twentieth-century studies of learning in animals. Ivan Pavlov's famous experiments showed how dogs would salivate when a bell rang, once the sound of the bell had been associated in their minds with food. This is called a conditioned response, and it is believed that phobias may be based on similar kinds of associations. As psychologists began to understand the basic rules of learning in animals, they realized how unwanted thought associations in phobic patients could be broken. Clinical psychology is constantly refining these methods so they will work more quickly and the patients will experience the minimum of anxiety.

BELOW Aversion therapy is a means of curing minor phobias by exposing the patient to whatever it is he or she is frightened of in a controlled environment so they can overcome their fears.

TOP LEFT Living in a world that was much less well-understood than it is now, fear would have been a useful protective mechanism for our ancient ancestors.

LEFT Spiders are one of the most common sources of phobias, though it is not clear why this should be.

Love and sex

M odern humans recognize the brain as the "source" of emotions such as love – but what about those infamous "hormones"? When scientists state that it's the brain that controls reproductive cycles in women and sperm production in men, they're not talking about the parts of the brain involved in thinking. They're referring to fundamental processes that keep those systems ticking, almost literally.

Ovaries and testes are kept in optimal condition by rhythmic stimulation from the pituitary gland. These pulses are initiated by hormones released from the hypothalamus approximately every hour. Controlling the endocrine glands by pulses of hormones is more efficient than constant stimulation (think how effectively a flashing light grabs your attention). Recent research shows that if these hormonal pulses stop, the ovaries or testes become inactive. This is what happens when the menstrual cycle stops in response to stress, anorexia, or breastfeeding.

The pulsing neurons that are responsible for ovulation are also the initiators of puberty. Once again, the brain is the leader, but this is no simple dictatorship. The hormones produced by the ovaries or testes are able to slip past the barriers that surround cells in the brain and compete for power. The complex interactions between the brain and steroids – the family of hormones able to penetrate the brain's defenses – are often discussed in terms of "feedback," since these interactions are mutually controlling and not always in balance.

The mechanisms in the brain regulating ovulation or sperm production are completely outside our conscious control – furthermore, there's no evidence to suggest that these hourly pulses have any impact on our emotional state. In contrast, the hormones released by the ovaries or testes, such as estrogen or testosterone, can have powerful effects on brain regions involved in mood regulation. Given such circumstances, it's far from clear which part of the body is in charge!

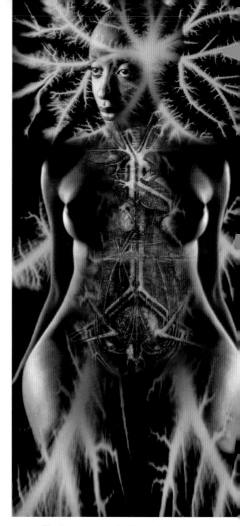

ABOVE The human reproductive system is managed automatically by the brain through rhythmic pulses of hormones that regulate ovulation and sperm production.

LOVE IS BLIND

Viewed as a series of chemical reactions, love is a form of madness. Lovers become obsessive, they suffer delusions, and they take an optimistic view of what the future holds, regardless of the facts. The chief culprit in this is believed to be oxytocin, a hormone released during sexual arousal that causes feelings of intimacy, but also temporarily disrupts the memory's store of previous experiences, resulting in the sensation of being detached from reality.

NEUROSCIENTISTS have yet to pinpoint the seat of love within the brain. As a complex emotion, however, love may be traceable to the limbic system, a group of neurons that is often considered to be the seat of our emotions (see pages 64–5). The neurons that form this system occur in areas such as the cingulate cortex, the hippocampus, the amygdala, and parts of the hypothalamus. They form an intricate, highly interconnected network, and disruption of the network often leads to emotional disturbances. By communicating with the hypothalamus, this circuit can influence both the physical and psychological aspects of emotions such as love.

From the scientific point of view, sex is a good deal simpler than love. The peripheral components of sex are controlled by the brain via the sympathetic and parasympathetic nervous systems – the same systems that control heart rate and some aspects of respiration (see pages 88–9). By releasing the neurotransmitter acetylcholine in the venous sphincters of the penis, a man's parasympathetic nervous system induces erection; the sympathetic release of another neurotransmitter, noradrenalin, in the vas deferens and seminal vessels then instigates ejaculation.

At a central level, orgasm induces the release of opioidlike peptides known as endorphins, which act on opiate receptors. These are the very same receptors that drugs such as morphine and heroin act on; and given the highly addictive nature of these drugs, it may be possible that people can become addicted to sex because of the psychological high produced by orgasm.

LIMBIC SYSTEM

CINGULATE GYRUS

OLFACTORY BULB

HYPOTHALAMUS

AMYGDALOID BODY

MAMMILLARY BODY

PARAHIPPOCAMPAL GYRUS

ABOVE The limbic system produces basic urges for things like food and sex. After the desire is answered, the limbic system releases endorphins that create a feeling of satisfaction.

BELOW Sex is relatively simple to explain if it is considered merely as a mechanical response to stimulation, but the feeling that we call love is not so easy to pin down to a specific set of neural activities.

ROMANTIC IDEALS AND CONCEPTS

RECOLLECTION OF PREVIOUS EXPERIENCES

SENSORY INPUTS – TOUCH, SMELL

PHYSICAL AROUSAL

The neurology of sex

*S*exual behavior is a combination of basic drives, hormonal regulation, and cultural conditioning. Humans are the only animals that divorce sex from simple reproduction, which means that the "higher" cognitive frontal lobes of the brain are involved as well as the automatic "need–response" areas.

MALE

FEMALE

RIGHT Basic sexual differences between males and females are established before we are born.

BELOW Sexual drives and responses depend on interactions between several areas of the brain: the amygdala evaluates whether an action is pleasant; the frontal cortex decides whether to perform an action; and the pituitary regulates the production of sex hormones.

Many of the differences between the sexes are controlled by the sexually dimorphic (SD) nucleus, in the front part of the hypothalamus. Normally this area grows much larger in males than in females – this happens in response to secretion of testosterone in the womb stimulated by the male fetus during the fourth month of pregnancy.

The neurons in this nucleus are activated during sexual arousal and intercourse. In male animals electrical stimulation of it promotes copulation, while damage to it reduces libido and performance. The SD nucleus therefore appears to be important for guiding male sexual behavior. However, we know that it doesn't control sex hormones directly, because injuries to it do not prevent the hypothalamus from producing the gonadotrophin-releasing hormones (GnRH) that in turn control the production of sex hormones by the pituitary gland. Nor do they inhibit the testes from producing testosterone.

In male homosexuals the SD nucleus tends to be smaller than normal, although they have normal levels of testosterone. Since many homosexuals have femalelike organization of the interconnections between the left and right speech areas of the brain, this suggests that the SD nucleus is responsible for some of the normal differences between male and female brains (*see pages 84–5*).

THE SEXUAL BRAIN

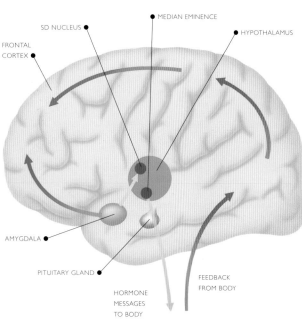

SD NUCLEUS

MEDIAN EMINENCE

FRONTAL CORTEX

HYPOTHALAMUS

AMYGDALA

PITUITARY GLAND

HORMONE MESSAGES TO BODY

FEEDBACK FROM BODY

Hormonal control

GnRH is released from another region of the hypothalamus, the median eminence. Interestingly, the neurons that synthesize GnRH aren't derived from the brain at all, but migrate to the hypothalamus from the olfactory system in the nose during the fourth month of pregnancy *(see pages 64–5)*. They then organize themselves to produce the pulses of GnRH that control the production of sex hormones.

System failure

Lying deep within the front part of the temporal lobe is the tiny almond-shaped nucleus called the amygdala *(see pages 76–7)*, which forms one of the main links between the hypothalamus and the rest of the brain. An animal with lesions of the amygdala becomes placid and tame and loses interest in sex. It seems that the amygdala's function is to associate scenes, events, or actions with their capacity to satisfy basic drives such as food, drink, sex, or self-preservation.

Part of the amygdala has a high density of testosterone receptors; it also has reciprocal connections with the SD nucleus. Any stimulation of this region in a male causes sexual arousal. Continued stimulation eventually leads to hypersexuality, so the animal will mount anything – even inanimate objects such as chairs. Occasionally an epileptic seizure stimulates this area in a human male, with equally bizarre effect.

Because the amygdala helps an animal to memorize useful behavior, it connects to the prefrontal part of the neocortex. This area is responsible for deciding what actions to perform, both for immediate gratification and with a view to their likely long-term benefits. Damage to the prefrontal cortex – which often occurs after road accidents – can result in socially unacceptable sexual behavior.

LEFT Viagra addresses the physical problems that produce impotence, but there is often an underlying psychological cause.

RIGHT The pleasure that we take from sexual intercourse has an obvious evolutionary benefit: the more sex we have, the more likely it is that our genes will survive.

IMPOTENCE

Male impotence is a common sexual problem. It is often assumed to be a symptom of neural failure, and yet the reflex actions of erection and ejaculation can still be experienced, although without pleasure, by a paraplegic whose spinal cord is intact though separated from the brain. In fact, the main cause of impotence is hardening of the arteries, which reduces the blood supply to the penis. The anti-impotence drug Viagra works by opening up the penile blood vessels, permitting the blood flow that makes erection possible.

Another common cause of impotence is psychological: a fear of failure that becomes self-fulfilling. Viagra can often overcome this problem, too, because it bypasses the neural control of the bulbospongiosus muscle, which normally controls tumescence, and so may succeed in breaking the vicious circle.

Gender and the brain

There are obvious differences in the bodies of men and women – but what about their brains? So far as size is concerned, women's brains are on average 15 percent smaller than men's, simply because women tend to be physically smaller than men. In addition, it's now well established that in certain brain regions the two sexes differ in terms of the density of neurons and their connections – a difference that has been observed in species ranging from rats to humans.

ABOVE The difference in average size between men and women is reflected in the average sizes of their brains.

Some of these regions are involved in reproductive processes, but sex differences are also noticeable at sites that contribute to other functions. For example, one particular part of the massive fiber bundle (the corpus callosum) that connects the two hemispheres of the brain is larger in women. This structural difference is particularly interesting, since it is in keeping with evidence suggesting that for certain tasks women make use of both sides of their brain to a greater extent than men do.

One effect of this is that women tend to have greater verbal facility than men, probably because speech is not so confined to the left hemisphere. Also, the relative bilaterality of women's speech helps protect it from damage, so that women are less likely than men to become dysphasic after left-hemisphere strokes. The better links between the two hemispheres may also make it easier for women to express the emotions represented in the right hemisphere. This may account for the way women seem to be "more in touch" with their emotions.

However, there is a cost to this verbal facility. Women are sometimes less well equipped visuospatially – a disadvantage for operations that require careful judgment of space, such as parking cars. But visuospatial skills are arguably less essential assets now than they were in prehistoric or medieval times, which may be one reason for the confusion many males feel about their role in the modern world.

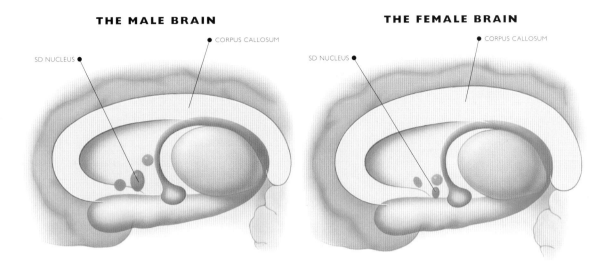

THE MALE BRAIN

SD NUCLEUS ●
● CORPUS CALLOSUM

THE FEMALE BRAIN

SD NUCLEUS ●
● CORPUS CALLOSUM

It should be emphasized that these sex differences are not completely genetic in origin. The genes set the biological background, but the differences only occur if the brain is exposed to hormones such as estrogen or testosterone. Consequently, the genetic gender can be overridden if there is a disturbance in the circulating level of those hormones early during development. In humans, this is probably restricted to the prenatal period. Once this critical phase has passed, it seems that the sex hormones are no longer able to affect the structure of the brain.

ABOVE The corpus callosum in female brains is more extensive than in males. These fibers connect the two brain hemispheres, so that the lateral specialization of brain function may be less pronounced in women than in men.

Are these differences significant?

In a world where there is an increasing focus on equality of opportunity, what is the likely reaction to the discovery of sex differences in the brain? It all depends! For example, studies in the 1990s in America and in Holland reported differences in the size of parts of the hypothalamus between homosexual and heterosexual men. The results were greeted with a sense of liberation in America – the reaction among the majority of the gay community being "nobody can blame us anymore, since homosexuality is in our nature" – but in Holland the response was "we feel demeaned, this research threatens our free will."

In fact, the reported differences between the sexes, and between homosexual and heterosexual men, are relatively subtle. Furthermore, the range of individual variation means that there is considerable overlap between the various groups. Although statistically men are on average taller than women, that doesn't preclude a huge number of exceptions; nor does it constitute a value judgment. Such differences provide something that a species loses at its peril – diversity.

ABOVE The political significance of brain research is obvious in Western societies that are increasingly concerned with issues of sexual equality.

Control systems

ABOVE If drought threatens, action has to be taken to monitor rainfall and make prompt contingency plans. In the same way, the brain monitors the condition of the body and takes action if its equilibrium is threatened in some way.

*T*he British Prime Minister Harold Macmillan was once asked what made governing a country difficult. "Events," he replied. Droughts, heatwaves, hemorrhages, hangovers – such "events" require complex responses in order to restore equilibrium. These particular crises put our body's water reserves in jeopardy. But water loss is rapidly detected, since our brains are constantly monitoring the concentration of the blood. One of the many responses is a change in our conscious state – an urgent thirst.

At the same time as the escalating thirst, and beyond our conscious awareness, the brain is releasing high levels of antidiuretic hormone (vasopressin), thereby commanding the kidneys to conserve water. The neurons that make this hormone are located in the hypothalamus, at the base of the brain. Fibers from those neurons project into the back of the pituitary gland – which lies just beneath the hypothalamus, behind the point where the optic nerves cross – and it is from this site that the hormone is discharged into the circulation.

As described earlier (*see pages 40–1*), homeostatic (balancing) processes are required to maintain our body temperature, our reserves of water and energy, and other vital functions, at the right level. In order for our bodies to enjoy optimal efficiency, these functions need to be maintained within tight margins. The hypothalamus monitors these parameters and activates compensatory responses, in much the

LEFT Like a thermostat, the brain monitors the condition of our bodies and takes the necessary steps to make sure our body systems are in balance.

HYPOTHALAMUS

BLOOD VESSELS FROM HYPOTHALAMUS

NERVE FIBERS TO POSTERIOR PART OF PITUITARY

PITUITARY GLAND

same way as a central-heating thermostat. Your temperature only has to diverge from normal by a few degrees for you to experience shivering or sweating. It's the hypothalamus that initiates these warning signs. It also initiates many other autonomic actions that are outside our conscious control, most of them beyond our conscious awareness.

The neuroendocrine system

The brain's ability to control remote organs via the bloodstream is called the neuroendocrine (brain/hormone) system. Apart from the antidiuretic hormone, there is only one other hormone that the brain secretes into circulation directly. This is oxytocin, the chemical messenger that stimulates milk ejection and uterine contractions. Its episodic release controls these events without our conscious participation.

A less direct effect on peripheral organs is achieved by another family of hormones made in the brain. Each of these has a unique role. The relevant hormone is released from the base of the hypothalamus into blood vessels that transport it to the front of the pituitary. Once there, it stimulates the release of an equivalent hormone that enters the bloodstream and targets a particular gland – such as the thyroid, adrenal, or testis – or growth sites in bones.

Although hormones play such vital roles, they are often damned as problem chemicals. Whenever the word "hormones" is mentioned, people tend to think of the fluctuations associated with the female reproductive cycle. It's certainly true that a few of them contribute to premenstrual tension and other menstrual problems: unfortunately we're burdened with a reproductive system that evolved when the female of the species was almost constantly pregnant or lactating, and therefore rarely exposed to these cyclic fluctuations. But despite the "bad press," we should remember that our lives depend on the vast orchestra of circulating hormones. In fact, they constitute one of just two ways in which the brain regulates the body: apart from making muscles move (the neuromuscular system), there is basically only one other way the brain can affect the rest of the body – and that is by bringing into play the neuroendocrine system.

The hypothalamus reminds us that the brain is not just an organ of thought, feeling, memory, and muscular action. An ability to cope with the potentially life-threatening "events" that challenge our vital functions is essential for our day-to-day survival. But this part of the brain is not exclusively committed to keeping bodily functions balanced – the hypothalamus is also the command center for many adventurous, non-homeostatic actions, including ovulation and childbirth (see pages 80–1).

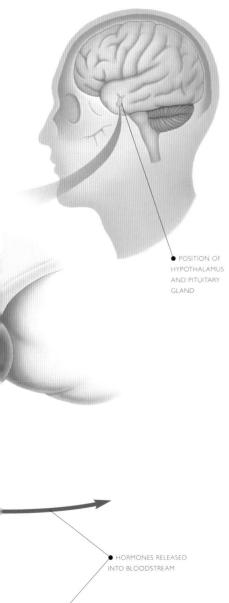

BELOW The hypothalamus and the pituitary gland are the most important agents in monitoring body systems and making adjustments by means of hormone release.

● POSITION OF HYPOTHALAMUS AND PITUITARY GLAND

● HORMONES RELEASED INTO BLOODSTREAM

Stress

In physiological terms, stress is the reaction induced by the perception of a threatening situation. The body's response involves two intrinsically linked systems: the autonomic nervous system and the pituitary–adrenal axis.

Unlike the skeletal muscle system, the autonomic nervous system is not under conscious control. It regulates many aspects of the visceral functions, including heart rate, blood pressure, and respiration, and the functioning of the sphincter, skin, blood vessels, pancreas, and liver. It involves a balance between two antagonistic networks: the sympathetic and the parasympathetic nervous systems.

The sympathetic nervous system is activated by stress. It releases the neurotransmitter noradrenalin, which increases heart rate and blood pressure and decreases intestinal activity, preparing the body for emergency action. This is known as the "fight or flight" response. Conversely, the parasympathetic system releases the neurotransmitter acetylcholine. This has the opposite effect on the visceral organs and is operative at times of stress-free quiescence.

ABOVE The symptoms of stress result from the body being made ready for action in response to a threat, like a spring being compressed. If the stress response is not discharged, the familiar problems of heart disease and gastric illness can result.

BELOW Information overload is often cited as one cause of stress. As the speed of communications increases, many office workers feel swamped with information that they have no time to process.

ADRENALIN

THE AUTONOMIC NERVOUS SYSTEM is under the control of the pituitary–adrenal axis. This consists of two structures that maintain a constant dialogue: the pituitary gland in the brain and the adrenal medulla. Under the control of the hypothalamus, the pituitary gland releases adrenocortical trophic hormone (ACTH), which promotes the secretory action of the adrenal gland (situated at one end of the kidney).

The adrenal gland has two parts, the medulla (inner part) and the cortex. The medulla releases adrenalin, while the cortex releases corticosteroids. Together these chemical messengers act on the sympathetic branch of the autonomic nervous system. The adrenalin stimulates the sympathetic neurons, while the corticosteroids promote catabolism (the conversion of sugars into energy); so between them, they boost the body's energy production to the level required to take action in response to emergencies.

The effects of stress

Prolonged uncontrollable stress can lead to serious ill-health, but in short bursts the stress reaction can be a lifesaver – especially in situations where it is possible to survive by physical exertion, by the so-called "fight or flight" response. In addition, stress hormones can reduce inflammation and immune responses, such as hayfever and other allergic reactions, and combat rejection in transplant patients. These benefits may have evolved partly as a short-term way to minimize the incapacitating effects of injury, regardless of the risk of subsequent infection. After all, if you are injured in a fight, your first priority is to win or escape.

Psychological experiments from the 1950s onward have attempted to explain why exposure to the same stressors can produce different results under different conditions. Stressful events that are capable of causing severe, sometimes fatal, gastric ulceration may under some circumstances produce no detectable ill effects at all. The outcome depends both on the individual experiencing the stress and on the circumstances under which it is experienced: painful events feel more painful and cause greater stress if they are uncontrollable and unpredictable.

Some personality types are susceptible to stress, while others are resilient. Early studies identified people with "Type A" personality – those who are impatient and competitive and constantly feel under time pressure – as being more likely to develop heart disease. Since then, it has been established that having a "Type A" personality does not necessarily mean a high risk of heart disease – one critical factor being whether or not you become angry and hostile when thwarted. More recently still, it has been shown that in animals – and perhaps in humans, too – prolonged high levels of stress hormones can cause brain cells to die. This is particularly clear in animals that have experienced unnaturally low levels of stress during early development. It seems as if the brain and the stress hormone system adjust one another's sensitivity during early life, with lasting consequences for the way we respond to stress as adults.

ABOVE Stress hormones can prevent immune responses like hayfever, which is a short-term way of improving your chances of escaping a threat.

ABOVE Time pressure is a common cause of stress symptoms, though the way we respond to stress will determine whether it has serious effects on our health.

Depression

ABOVE Clinical depression is a very much more severe affliction than the occasional periods of unhappiness that affect most people at one time or another.

All of us are prone to bouts of melancholia, particularly after harrowing events such as bereavement – but clinical depression is a more severe condition. In addition to the more familiar symptoms (low self-esteem, sleep disturbance, loss of motivation, and feelings of misery), there may be psychotic symptoms such as hallucinations and delusions.

We still do not know for certain how depression is triggered, nor exactly how the various antidepressant drugs work. However, there is a strong possibility that depression is a result of low levels of monoamine neurotransmitters in the brain. Reserpine, a drug that depletes the brain of stores of monoamine neurotransmitters, can trigger depression; conversely, depression can often be alleviated by amine-uptake inhibitors (see below).

However, despite the evidence, there are problems with this theory. One is that typical antidepressant drugs increase neurotransmitter levels rapidly, but the effects are only discernible after a matter of weeks. What is more, some of the "atypical" antidepressants do not block amine uptake at all; and cocaine, a potent amine uptake blocker, has no antidepressant effects. There is therefore both corroboratory and contradictory evidence for the monoamine theory, and so far nobody has been able either to prove or disprove it or to come up with a convincing alternative.

Treatment

Mild to moderate depression often responds to placebo treatment or psychotherapy. More severe attacks are usually treated with drugs or, in extreme cases, with electroconvulsive therapy. Antidepressant drugs are divided into three classes: amine-uptake inhibitors, monoamine-oxidase inhibitors, and atypical antidepressants.

LEFT Bipolar depression is characterized by wild swings between mania and despair.

LITHIUM

Lithium therapy is used for both unipolar and bipolar depression. A naturally occurring metal, initially it took time to catch on – partly because of the reluctance of the pharmaceutical industry to research and market a drug that could not be patented. It is now one of the mainstays of modern treatment.

The amine-uptake inhibitors are all tricyclic drugs (so-called because of their three-ringed molecular structure). They inhibit the body's uptake of amines by drawing them back into the nerve terminals from which they were released. However, because they block a variety of receptors, they tend to have side effects. Fewer side effects are generally encountered with the newer, selective drugs, such as Prozac, that block uptake of the monoamine neurotransmitter 5-HT only.

Monoamine-oxidase inhibitors block the degradation of the monoamines in the neurons that release them, so that a larger pool is available for release. But these compounds have unwanted side effects, too, and they are not as widely prescribed as uptake blockers.

The atypical antidepressants have little effect on amine uptake; it may be that they reduce the negative feedback that operates on neurotransmitter release, thus increasing the levels of amine released. These compounds have fewer side effects than the other two groups, but seem to be effective only in the short term.

ECT

Electroconvulsive therapy (ECT) involves stimulating the brain through electrodes attached to the scalp. ECT has been shown to be as effective as drug treatments, if not more so. Although it can cause confusion and memory loss that may last for weeks, it is the most successful treatment for severe, suicidal depression.

TYPES OF DEPRESSION

THERE ARE TWO TYPES of depressive syndrome: unipolar and bipolar. The unipolar variety is characterized by persistent episodes of depression. Women are twice as likely as men to suffer from it, and there is a moderate genetic risk factor. With bipolar depression, on the other hand, the sufferer swings between depression and a state of mania. In the manic state, the sufferer displays excessive excitement and energy, which can lead to wild extravagance and impulsiveness. The duration of the periods of depression and mania can vary enormously, from hours to years, sometimes alternating with clockwork regularity. There is a significant genetic predisposition toward manic depression, with an equal risk factor for both sexes.

LEFT Depression is often seen as the scourge of modern Western society and is attributed to various causes from the decline of communal values to a sense of lacking control.

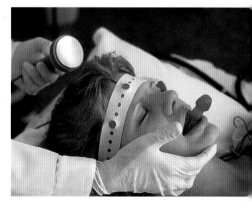

RIGHT Electroconvulsive therapy is a direct, and some would argue unsophisticated, method of breaking a depressive cycle.

Caffeine, nicotine, and alcohol

The three most widely used drugs – caffeine, nicotine, and alcohol – have been accepted or tolerated by many societies for hundreds of years. But both nicotine and alcohol are highly addictive and, in terms of damage to health and destruction of people's lives, constitute as great a social ill as more notorious and hence illegal drugs such as cocaine and heroin.

Caffeine

One of a class of drugs known as the methylxanthines, caffeine is an ingredient of many beverages, including coffee, tea, cocoa, and many soft drinks. It is also an ingredient in a variety of over-the-counter pills and preparations. Caffeine stimulates the central nervous system, giving improved concentration, increased mental awareness, increased alertness, a clearer flow of thought, and a reduction in fatigue. But it also causes stimulation of the heart, relaxation of smooth muscle, particularly in the airways of the lungs, and an increase in urine production. At higher doses, it induces restlessness, tremors, agitation, and disruption of the cardiac rhythm.

Caffeine works by increasing the level of an excitatory intracellular messenger called cyclic AMP. Its stimulatory effects are much milder than those of amphetamines, and the subsequent period of depression is decreased accordingly. There are signs that caffeine can induce some degree of physical dependency, though this is certainly not severe. Although caffeine itself has no clinical uses, theophylline, one of the other methylxanthines, is used as a bronchodilator because of its relaxing effects on the smooth muscle of the lungs.

LEFT Caffeine, alcohol, and nicotine are so widely used and accepted that many people scarcely regard them as drugs at all, but they all have well-documented detrimental effects.

Nicotine

Nicotine is the only pharmacologically active substance in tobacco smoke, although the carcinogenic tars and carbon monoxide have other, more lethal, effects. It appears to act on the central nervous system in two ways, depending on the strength of the dose. At low strengths, nicotine mimics the neurotransmitter acetylcholine. This leads to stimulation of the brain, causing changes in electrical activity. At this level, nicotine increases performance under stress, which is why it appears to alleviate stress symptoms. At higher doses, however, nicotine becomes a depressant, producing a blocking or desensitizing effect by binding to the acetylcholine receptors.

Apart from its effects on the brain, nicotine can increase heart rate and blood pressure, as well as reducing bowel motility and appetite. When nicotine is inhaled along with the tars and carbon monoxide in tobacco smoke, the effects are seriously damaging, increasing the risk of lung cancer, leukemia, coronary heart disease, and chronic bronchitis. Although these facts are well known, smoking remains common partly because nicotine is so addictive – on a scale comparable with heroin and cocaine. Because of the degree of physical and psychological dependence, people who give up smoking often suffer severe withdrawal symptoms, such as irritability, impaired performance of tasks, and sleep disturbance.

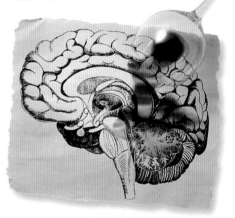

BELOW Like many depressants, if alcohol is taken in large enough quantities, it can lead to coma and death.

Alcohol

Alcohol is perhaps the most misused drug. Directly and indirectly, its abuse leads to many thousands of deaths each year. The major effects of alcohol consumption are on the central nervous system, where it has a considerable depressant effect. There are three possible mechanisms by which this occurs: it can inhibit transmitter release from nerve terminals, depress cells by interacting with the GABA "A" receptor *(see pages 96–7)*, and can also inhibit the functioning of the glutamate receptor (glutamate being the major excitatory neurotransmitter).

LEFT Because nicotine is highly addictive, giving up smoking produces the same kind of withdrawal symptoms as those suffered by people who stop using so-called hard drugs such as cocaine or heroin.

Cocaine and amphetamines

Cocaine and amphetamines are the most widely used central stimulants. Although their origins and history are very different, their effects are remarkably similar. Both kinds of drug stimulate the brain, causing increased intellectual activity and euphoria. Physical performance is enhanced, giving a sense of greater energy and less fatigue. Both are able to suppress appetite, a use that has given amphetamines a niche in the treatment of obesity. They are also useful tools for studying the reward pathways in the brain, because of their apparent ability to increase the levels at which these pathways work.

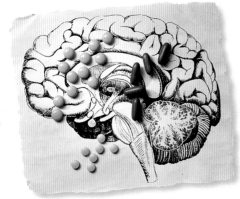

ABOVE The brain is very susceptible to chemical interference, which is why "recreational" drugs have such dramatic effects, and also why they are potentially so dangerous.

Cocaine

A substance that occurs naturally in the leaves of the South American coca shrub, cocaine was first used by the Incas, in Peru, and other Andean tribes. They discovered that chewing the leaves allowed them to do strenuous work with little sign of fatigue, particularly at high altitudes.

The pharmacological action of cocaine is very simple. It blocks the reuptake of the nerotransmitter dopamine into nerve terminals, so there is more dopamine available to excite the postsynaptic neurons. This produces the sense of euphoria and confidence associated with the drug. Cocaine was not considered an especially dangerous drug early in this century, as is indicated by the fact that the fictional detective Sherlock Holmes took cocaine to alleviate boredom between cases. Sigmund Freud eulogized the properties of the drug for a wide range of afflictions, until its damaging effects became apparent. Severe depression is experienced when the effects of the drug wear off; as a result, although cocaine does not appear to cause physical dependence, it is easy to become psychologically addicted to it.

Cocaine is often taken in the form of a hydrochloride salt, which is either inhaled or injected intravenously. It can also be dissolved in ether, or mixed with baking soda and then smoked as "crack." This exposes the entire surface area of the lungs to the drug, rather than just the nasal area; as a result, it gives a bigger, though shorter, "high" and is followed by greater depression. For this reason, crack is considerably more addictive than inhaled or injected cocaine.

AMPHETAMINES

AMPHETAMINES have a very different history. Amphetamine was first synthesized in 1887, but it was not until 1927, during a search for a new anti-asthma drug, that its psychotic effects were noted. Initially amphetamines were marketed as nasal sprays for asthma and as oral treatments for narcolepsy (an abnormal desire to sleep). Subsequently they were prescribed for chronic fatigue and for weight control. By the late 1950s their negative qualities were becoming apparent, prompting legislation to control their distribution.

The way amphetamines work stems from their structural similarity to the neurotransmitters noradrenalin and dopamine. They increase the levels of these transmitters in the synapse by blocking the reuptake mechanisms (in the same way as cocaine) and displacing the transmitters from their stores within the nerve terminal.

The behavioral effects of amphetamines seem to be caused mainly by the increased dopamine release. Dopamine is thought to play a central role in the reward pathways governing feelings, and an increase in the levels of this transmitter could explain the high that these stimulants induce. The same effect is also induced by "ecstasy" (methylene-dioxymethamphetamine, or MDMA). This has mixed stimulant and hallucinogenic properties, due to the way it increases both dopamine and 5-HT (the 5-HT system being the one targeted by the hallucinogens).

ABOVE The "high" experienced by drug users results from the increased levels of dopamine, the pleasure neurotransmitter, that drugs like cocaine and ecstasy produce in the brain.

DRUG DEPENDENCE

There are two aspects to drug addiction: physical and psychological. Generally, physical dependence follows a developed tolerance to a drug, so that increasingly large amounts are required to produce the same effects; if the user stops taking the drug, then the body ceases to function normally and withdrawal symptoms are experienced. Psychological dependence stems from a craving for the drug, a desire to continue taking it in order to experience the "high," or other effects, that the drug produces.

ABOVE The damaging social effects of illegal drug use among young people especially have provoked much debate in the West as to the best way to solve the problems of addiction and drug crime.

Anxiety

*A*nxiety is a condition that plagues many people, and yet it is one of the hardest
afflictions to diagnose clinically. It is often difficult to distinguish between a
"normal" state of anxiety – an integral part of human life that serves as a driving
force for many of our actions – and a "pathological" state requiring treatment.
Despite this ambiguity, some five to ten percent of the world's population are diagnosed as sufferers; and anxiolytics (drugs used to treat anxiety) and hypnotics (sleep
inducers) are among the most widely prescribed modern drugs.

BELOW Anxiety is part of normal life,
serving as a stimulus to action, but
extreme anxiety can cause symptoms
such as hyperventilation, hot flushes,
and cardiac problems.

Anxiety has both mental and physical symptoms. It induces a
subjective sensation, very similar to fear or terror, so that the sufferer lives in a constant state of uneasiness, as if expecting some
imminent catastrophe. The physical symptoms include cardiac
complaints caused by inappropriate stimulation of the heart by
the brain. Sometimes a vicious circle develops, with anxiety leading to heart trouble, which then leads to further anxiety, and so
on. Someone suffering from severe anxiety shows hyperventilation, a flushed face, and profuse perspiration.

Barbiturates and benzodiazepines

As with most psychiatric disorders, psychotherapy and drug
therapy are the mainstays of treatment. Psychotherapy can play
a greater role in treating anxiety than it does in treating
afflictions such as schizophrenia. However, drug treatment remains a powerful tool, one that is used by many
millions worldwide. Anxiolytic drugs work mainly by
increasing the action of the inhibitory neurons in the
brain that release a neurotransmitter known as GABA
(gamma-amino butyric acid), which produces a sedative
effect. The two major categories of anxiolytic drugs, the
barbiturates and the benzodiazepines, both interact with
the "A class" of GABA receptors, increasing the inhibition of the cells that these receptors lie on.

Barbiturates were developed in the early part of the
twentieth century. They bind to the GABA "A" receptor
and increase the duration of response to GABA itself.

KEEPING BUSY

The old-fashioned advice that you should keep yourself occupied in the face of worries and anxiety has some validity in terms of the way our brains work. This is partly to do with the lateralization of the brain that was discussed earlier (see pages 52–3). The right side of the brain is, broadly speaking, responsible for our emotional responses, particularly feelings of anxiety or sorrow. Engaging in some kind of left-brain activity such as reading, talking, doing the crossword, or playing chess will tend to inhibit the activity of the moody right hemisphere. Focusing on non-emotional mental tasks also has the effect of damping down the activity of the amygdala, part of the limbic system that produces feelings of fear and distress.

Discussing your worries might be helpful because, in the process of rationalizing them, you gain some left-brain control over them and they cease to be so emotionally overwhelming.

ABOVE Anxiety is an essential response to dangers of one kind or another. If we never became anxious, we would not respond appropriately to a threat.

Barbiturates are more depressant than benzodiazepines (which have now largely replaced them), because at higher doses they can initiate a response from the receptor directly, without the need for GABA binding. For this reason, barbiturates have a small "window" of concentrations at which they are therapeutically useful. Higher concentrations can be fatal.

Benzodiazepines such as diazepam (Valium) and temazepam act on the same receptor, but at a different site. They increase the frequency of reception in the presence of GABA, but cannot directly cause the receptor to act. They therefore have greater selectivity and are much safer. At low doses they are more anxiolytic than sedative, and even a serious overdose is likely to result in nothing more than deep sleep. They have therefore become the drug of choice both among doctors and patients.

ABOVE Anxiety is different from fear in that it often has no obvious cause. It can produce feelings of helplessness because the sufferer cannot identify what it is that is causing the feeling of unease.

ANXIETY AND 5-HT

THERE IS ANOTHER GROUP of anxiolytic drugs that acts on a particular subclass of 5-hydroxytryptamine (5-HT) receptors, which control the amount of the neurotransmitter 5-HT released. Further varieties of these drugs have been introduced that block postsynaptic 5-HT receptors, with the same effect. This group of drugs has been shown to have a purer anxiolytic effect than the benzodiazepines, producing fewer side effects.

It would appear from the effect of these drugs that 5-HT plays a key role in anxiety – but, as with the role of 5-HT in depression (see pages 90–1), there has so far been no corroborating evidence put forward to explain precisely what this is.

Opiates and opioids

The best-known category of drugs used for relieving severe pain are the narcotics, which are divided into two categories: opiates and opioids. Chemicals that can mimic the effects of opium are classed as opioids, whereas opiates have structures actually resembling that of opium. Opium itself contains morphine, the basis of many synthetic derivatives, among them heroin and codeine.

ABOVE Morphine was used extensively to treat wounded soldiers during the First World War, although its addictive properties were not then well known.

Pain relief

Morphine and the other opiates act at one of three receptors to inhibit cells. They reduce sensitivity to most types of pain, as well as decreasing the "affective" component of pain, making it easier to bear – so patients who are under the influence of morphine sometimes say they can feel the pain but that it does not matter. The analgesic effect is caused by an interaction with the pain pathways at spinal cord level, while the affective component is thought to act on the limbic system, the part of the brain believed to be responsible for emotions. The balance between the two components is not the same for all opiates – some are highly effective at inhibiting pain, but seem to have few central effects on the limbic system.

The opiate receptors also respond to endorphins and enkephalins, which occur naturally in the body. These peptides affect the intensity with which pain messages are received, and it has been suggested that opiates stimulate their release – thus producing analgesic effects.

Euphoria and nausea

The way an opiate works depends on the balance of its action on two types of receptor, known as μ receptors and κ receptors. Morphine, for example, produces a sense of wellbeing, or euphoria, which appears to be mediated via the μ receptors – whereas activation of the κ receptors leads to the opposite effect, depression or dysphoria.

Morphine also causes respiratory depression, due to its effect on receptors in the medulla oblongata, the part of the brainstem that contains the control centers for the heart and lungs. This is the principal cause of deaths from opiate poisoning. However, opiates also decrease the cough reflex and cause nausea and vomiting, due to their effect on an area of the medulla oblongata called the chemoreceptor trigger zone. Since many other drugs cause vomiting, too, it is thought that the purpose of this reaction is to prevent poisoning due to consumption of noxious substances. Although morphine remains our most potent analgesic and is widely used for pain relief, because of these side effects, therapeutic doses have to be carefully monitored.

LEFT The popularity of high-risk activities such as bungee jumping might be due to their stimulating release of the body's natural painkillers.

BELOW Sensations of pain are transmitted to the brain from the injured area via the spinal cord; opiates can disrupt the pain pathways through the spinal cord.

ADDICTION

REPEATED USE of morphine and other opiates rapidly leads to physical and psychological dependence, probably due to the activation of an excitatory mechanism that comes into play to balance the inhibition caused by the opiate. When the opiate is withdrawn, there is nothing to balance the extra excitation; this results in the withdrawal symptoms known as "cold turkey," which include sweating, irritability, aggression, and flulike symptoms. There are some useful antagonists, such as naloxone, that counteract the effects of opiates; these can be used to reverse narcotic overdoses and for treating heroin dependence.

In addition to the well-attested forms of addiction, there is the possibility that people can become addicted to the reactions of their endogenous endorphins and enkephalins – which may account for phenomena such as "jogger's high" and an enthusiasm for high-risk activities such as parachuting.

PAIN PATHWAYS

The pain receptors in various parts of the body send axons into the spinal cord. Here, within the dorsal horn, they synapse onto fibers that project into the brain. There are also descending pathways from the brain that can modulate these synapses and so alter their strength. Opiates work both at the spinal cord level, where they inhibit the neurons projecting into the brain, and centrally in the brain itself.

There are two types of pain fibers: some send information about fast pain, some about slow pain. Opiates act only on those involved with slow pain.

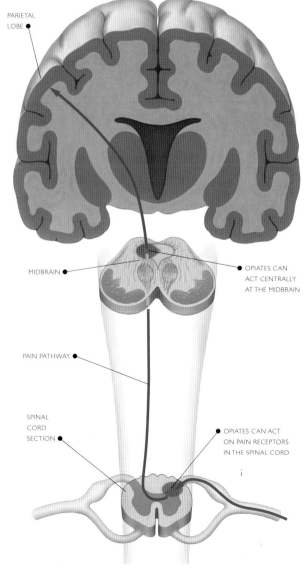

PARIETAL LOBE

MIDBRAIN

OPIATES CAN ACT CENTRALLY AT THE MIDBRAIN

PAIN PATHWAY

SPINAL CORD SECTION

OPIATES CAN ACT ON PAIN RECEPTORS IN THE SPINAL CORD

Sleep

What is sleep? Some scientists regard it as one extreme of a continuum of arousal, the other extreme being complete disorganization. In the past it was regarded as a "lapse" of the brain due to insufficient sensory stimulation, but it is now clear that the story is much more complex than this.

Most of our information about sleep, and about the patterns of sleep in particular, comes from electroencephalograms (EEGs) that measure the activity of the brain cells via electrodes placed on the scalp. These EEGs show that during normal sleep the cells fire in synchrony, and during the course of synchronized (S) sleep, this synchrony increases as sleep becomes deeper. However, there is also a state of what is known as paradoxical sleep, where EEGs show the cells firing in a fast, desynchronized manner – much as they do during wakefulness, although the hippocampus remains synchronized. During this desynchronized (D) sleep, sleepers lose all muscle tone, show rapid eye movement (REM), and are very difficult to wake. It is during this period that we dream.

ABOVE AND RIGHT Different stages of the sleep cycle produce different responses in our bodies. During REM sleep, when dreaming takes place, the sleeper is almost completely paralyzed and difficult to wake. At other stages the sleeper may move around and be easily awakened.

BIOLOGICAL RHYTHMS

Most organisms, from single cells to humans, are equipped with a built-in 24-hour clock. As a result, even when deprived of the light-dark cycle, they exhibit a daily rhythm. When humans spend a long period alone in a cave without a clock or any other time cues, they still show a daily rhythm of sleep, alertness, body temperature, urine production, and other functions. This cycle is remarkably regular, but it is usually a little longer than 24 hours (we don't know why). Consequently, when such cave dwellers return to the surface after many months, they underestimate the number of days that have passed. Biological rhythms of this kind are called circadian rhythms – from Latin, meaning "approximately a day."

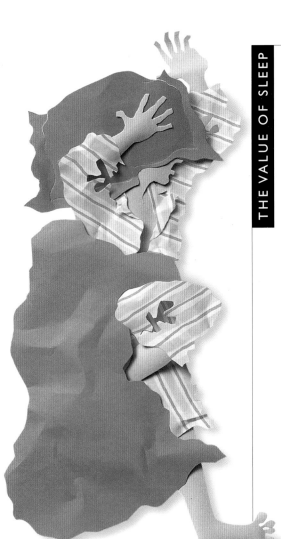

THE VALUE OF SLEEP

WHY WE NEED SLEEP has still not been fully explained, although some facts have been deduced from the effects of sleep deprivation. Since this has no effect on physiological performance and yet greatly impairs cognitive performance, S sleep is thought to be related to brain metabolic restoration. In other words, it "refreshes" the brain.

Although all vertebrates show S sleep, D sleep has been detected only in mammals and birds. It appears to be needed to consolidate new learning. As the hippocampus is one of the areas of the brain involved in learning, this may account for the increased levels of the neurotransmitter acetylcholine that reach the hippocampus during D sleep.

This may also explain why children need more sleep than adults do. The majority of newborn babies spend 50 percent of their sleeping time in D sleep; and the percentage is even higher in the case of babies born prematurely. But by the age of ten, the amount of time devoted to D sleep decreases to 25 percent, and it remains at that level until well into old age. Since childhood is the period when we acquire most information and learning, that could be the reason why we need so much D sleep during the earliest part of our life.

BRAIN ACTIVITY DURING S SLEEP ●

BRAIN ACTIVITY DURING D SLEEP ●

RIGHT An electroencephalogram can give a reading of a person's brain activity during the sleep cycle from the early stages of sleep to deep sleep and REM (dreaming) sleep.

We now know the precise site of the body clock. It consists of a few thousand neurons clustered together in the hypothalamus, at the base of the brain, just above the point where the optic nerves cross. This location makes sense – because some of the fibers projecting from the eyes connect with the clock. We benefit from this when flying across time zones, since the clock is able to adjust to the new cycle by about 90 minutes per day. Recent research has shown that the hormone melatonin can sometimes help to accelerate the shift to the new cycle, though no reliable evidence has been adduced for the life-enhancing claims that have also been made on melatonin's behalf.

FAR LEFT An internal clock, working to a 24-hour rhythm, is a fundamental mechanism of almost all living creatures, including human beings.

chapter four

the adult brain

The adult brain is completely personalized, a unique product of genetic inheritance and lived experience that governs every aspect of our social and creative activities.

The Adult Brain
introduction

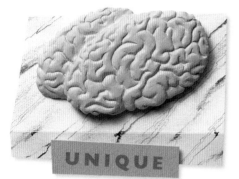

UNIQUE

ABOVE Not just any old piece of meat, each person's adult brain is a uniquely personalized mechanism – a mind that draws on our experience as well as our genetic inheritance.

By the time we reach adulthood, we are truly individual. Our genes will have interacted with our idiosyncratic experiences to produce not just a functioning brain, but a very personalized brain – a mind. One of the biggest questions that neuroscientists have to answer is how and where the brain becomes a mind. Many of the early theories about the brain placed our basic drives to create and destroy at the bottom of the human repertoire, and went to some lengths to explain how these drives were accommodated and realized by "higher" levels of organization within the brain.

Some of the earlier theorists – such as Sigmund Freud, with his concepts of the "ego" and "id" – were reluctant to relate these ideas of a hierarchy of control to the brain itself. With the benefit of several more decades of research, later psychologists and neuroscientists, such as Paul Maclean, focused on different structures in the brain, corresponding to different levels of organization.

Nowadays, the brain is no longer thought of as being divided into feelings on the one hand and logical thought on the other. And it has turned out to be much more difficult than anyone ever imagined to interpret in brain terms what we mean by concepts such as "intelligence." Just as no brain region is the control center "for" any particular function, so there are no "levels" in how functions are realized.

RIGHT Despite some limited correlations, we can't make a straightforward map of the brain, attributing different functions to different areas.

ABOVE However similar the faces in a crowd, each person is an individual island of consciousness, with unique talents, pleasures, intelligences, and fears.

This issue becomes particularly difficult, and particularly intriguing, when we begin to explore how different types of intelligence and creativity are present in different people in different ways and to different extents.

Personality

All brains look pretty much the same to the naked eye: there are no clues given by the macro brain structures as to where personality or specific talents are generated. Forty or fifty years ago, it was fairly common practice to perform invasive brain surgery in an effort to map out the brain, and to deal with any sections that seemed to have gone wrong. Modern brain imaging techniques have rendered this kind of surgery obsolete, but being able to see how sections of the brain "light up" when particular functions are being performed does not answer all the questions we still have.

One way we can discover more about the physical basis of personality is to investigate what happens in the brain when personality appears to be aberrant. In this chapter we shall look at the effects of tumors and brain damage on personality; and, conversely, examine how problems such as autism and schizophrenia are related to aberrations in brain organization and chemistry.

We shall see that there is no brain region, nor any chemical, "for" personality. Instead the personalization of our brains, with our own particular portfolio of talents and proclivities, seems to be a feature of a more global brain function, where a variety of factors play an important role. Above all, we shall see that personality can never be a static phenomenon – because we go on evolving as people as we live our lives. Indeed, the dynamism of the brain that enables us to benefit from the environment as we grow up continues to be active throughout our adult life and into old age, even following severe disruption by accidents or illness.

RIGHT Despite the dying cells and slipping memories, an active brain continues to develop into old age: effectively, creatively, sharply, using all its experience.

Theories about the brain

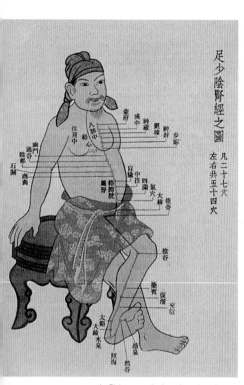

ABOVE A Chinese painting showing the acupuncture points. The head does not have any points mapped, reflecting the ancient Chinese medical view that mental faculties were located in organs other than the brain.

It seems quite obvious to us that our consciousness, thoughts, and feelings are all located in our head, behind our eyes, and that our brain is the center of our being. However, this was not at all self-evident to people in the past.

Ancient Chinese medicine had no role for the brain and located thought in the spleen. Ancient Egyptian medicine also located all mental and spiritual faculties in the major organs, such as the heart, liver, and kidneys. Indeed, in most ancient belief systems there was no place for the brain, and the heart was most commonly seen as the center of feeling. This changed with the ancient Greeks, who appreciated the importance of the brain, although even Aristotle visualized it as a form of glorified refrigerator that cooled the liquid "humors" originating from the major organs. In the West, our modern understanding of the brain started with the so-called Scientific Revolution at the end of the Middle Ages.

Each age has sought to understand the brain by analogy with contemporary technology. Early Western medicine saw the brain and nervous system as a network of tubes conducting fluids. In the nineteenth century, the brain was seen as a kind of telephonic switchboard, with our consciousness as a "ghost in the machine" examining messages from the various departments of the nervous system. More recently, the brain has been seen as a kind of digital computer.

ABOVE Aristotle (382–322 BCE), scientist, physician, and philosopher, was one of the first to write extensively on human thought.

ABOVE How well can we communicate the workings of our minds? Discourse, counseling, analysis, and therapy represent one extensive arena of study.

PSYCHOTHERAPY TODAY

HOW DO WE TREAT PSYCHOLOGICAL DISORDERS

today? Cognitive psychological methods are particularly good for treating panic and specific phobias. They can also help with some mood disorders, often in combination with drug treatments. These methods have very different foundations from the psychoanalytic traditions, and do not disrupt the patient's life.

Their aim is to help the patient to think differently. For example, for sufferers from depression everything seems to confirm their feelings of worthlessness: if an acquaintance fails to greet them in the street, that means they aren't likable. With cognitive psychotherapy, patients have to do "homework" – such as going over all the possible reasons why someone might fail to say hello in the street. Perhaps the other person was preoccupied? Or depressed? Or near-sighted? This way, patients can retrain their habits of thought, so they stop viewing their daily experiences as confirmations of failure or worthlessness. Such "retraining" has to be worked at: there's no evidence that simply telling patients that their attitude is at fault does any good, and it can make matters worse.

Despite successes in treating fears and phobias, cognitive methods have so far made little progress in treating conditions like schizophrenia, where psychiatry and drug treatments are still the norm. Nevertheless, as our understanding of the underlying neural bases for these conditions increases, we may hope for a synergy between psychiatry, psychology, and neurology that will lead to more effective forms of treatment.

Darwin's theory of evolution has also been applied to the brain. In the 1930s the American neuroscientist Paul Maclean suggested that the form of the human brain was due to the evolutionary superimposition of different "animal" brains – the primitive reptilian brain (the limbic system), the mammalian brain, and finally "neomammalian" brain (responsible for language, mathematics, and other specifically human abilities).

More modern theories stress the adaptability and interconnectedness of the human brain, and see theories such as Maclean's as excessively hierarchical. In recent years Gerald Edelman has argued that a given individual's brain evolves with experience and time, just as animal species have evolved and adapted over millions of years. Although the brain has specialized regions, it ultimately functions as a whole and cannot be reduced to simple components, like a car. If it is a "machine," it is unlike any machine that any of us have ever come across before – and this makes it extraordinarily difficult to find the language with which even to begin to describe it.

RIGHT Treating mental disorders by drilling holes in the patient's skull has thankfully been superseded by more sophisticated techniques.

Intelligence

Man, so we are told, has achieved his present evolutionary status because of his intelligence; prehistoric man was "backward" because he lacked intelligence. We often assume that successful members of society are the intelligent ones, whereas the failures and drop-outs are in some way deficient. What is this desirable quality that makes us what we are, and enables us to achieve varying degrees of success in the world?

ABOVE The notion of the "survival of the fittest" centers on adaptability, which in turn is often equated with intelligence or at least ingenuity.

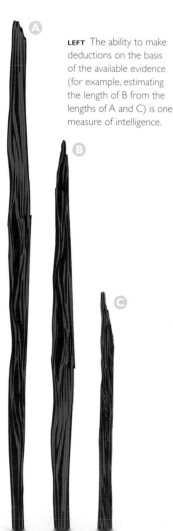

LEFT The ability to make deductions on the basis of the available evidence (for example, estimating the length of B from the lengths of A and C) is one measure of intelligence.

The term "intelligence" is often used as if it referred to something objective that people can have more or less of. In fact, intelligence is more like a skill than an object. Just as possession of a muscle does not guarantee its effective use, so knowledge has to be carefully analyzed and coordinated if it is to be used intelligently. Intelligence is not simply the ability to store facts; it also implies the ability to use facts appropriately.

At this level of generality, a definition of intelligence presents no serious problems. But when we try to define more precisely the skills and processes that make up "intelligence," we run into difficulties. A multitude of definitions have been offered: a capacity for abstract thought; the ability to adapt to relatively new situations; the capacity to learn or to profit by experience; or, tautologically, the ability to do well in intelligence tests.

There is no doubt, for example, that adults are generally cleverer than children. Present a five-year-old child with two sticks, A and B, of unequal length, and ask which is the longer. He or she will correctly answer A. Next, offer two further sticks, B and C, also of unequal length, and repeat the question. Back will come the correct answer B. But then if you ask which of A and C is the longer stick, the chances are that the answer will be wrong. Yet to the majority of adults, the correct answer is obvious. So is the development of intelligence just a matter of experience?

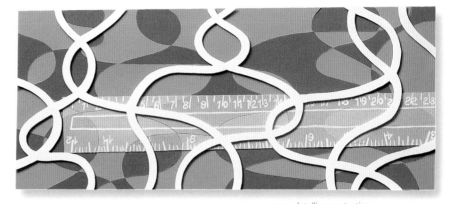

SOME PSYCHOLOGISTS have suggested that we are born with a specific level of intelligence that limits our potential for intellectual development. Furthermore, they argue that this intelligence quotient (IQ) is governed by genetic factors, our IQ being largely determined by the interaction of our parents' genes. This implies that, broadly speaking, intelligent parents will produce intelligent children, and less able parents produce less able children. In other words, that intelligence is a capacity passed down from one generation to the next. In the most general sense, this claim is indisputable: our basic human capacity to think and reason is inherited from our ancestors, just as we inherit the ability to walk or to see. However, a corollary of this view is that although the environment in which we grow up can help us to achieve our innate intellectual potential, it cannot take us beyond that limit.

TWIN STUDIES

Some of the most convincing evidence for the heritability of intelligence concerns the study of identical twins, since they possess identical genetic inheritance. Typical estimates suggest that 80 percent of an individual's intellectual capacity is determined by heredity, while only 20 percent of the variation between individuals is determined by the environment. On this basis, identical twins should exhibit an overwhelming similarity in intellectual skills, irrespective of their background or upbringing. In particular, given the overwhelming influence of inheritance as compared to environment, identical twins reared apart should show greater similarity in intelligence than non-identical twins reared together.

However, the value of some twin studies has been questioned. One criticism is that investigators have not sufficiently taken into account the phenomenon of "selective placement" – that is, the tendency of adoption and fostering agencies to place separated twins in homes of similar quality.

ABOVE Intelligence testing is often criticized for being simplistic, or culturally biased, or as trying to measure the unmeasurable, like using a ruler in water.

BELOW One problem with intelligence tests is their inability to span the range and variety of intelligent thought and action.

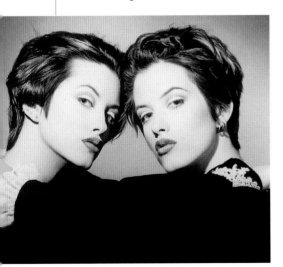

LEFT Twins together. The shared genetic inheritance of identical twins is a source of constant fascination and an ever-growing mountain of research.

IQ tests

The procedures generally used to "evaluate" intelligence rely on standardized IQ tests to measure various forms of ability. The standard is based on the premise that the tests – which consist of a variety of problems, such as verbal and spatial skills – have been administered to a large number of individuals from a homogeneous socioeconomic background and then adjusted so a distribution of scores is obtained, with the greatest number of individuals scoring in the middle range.

ABOVE Our genetic background is the key to our intelligence, but its development and flourishing is dependent on more intangible social factors.

RIGHT Like father, like son: lifestyles as well as genes are passed down through generations, so it is no surprise if a child's talents reflect its parents'.

However, an IQ score is by no means an absolute measure. Through the test standardization, the individual's score is relative to what other individuals from a broadly similar background may expect to score. But there are two problems with this procedure. First, the test may be inappropriate for a particular individual because his background is very different from those on whom the test was standardized. To take an extreme example, since certain African tribes are unaccustomed to perspective cues in line drawings, any test that incorporates these features would be an inappropriate measure of their intellectual capacity. For this reason IQ tests need to take into account the cultural background of the person tested, and "culture-free" tests have been devised for just this purpose.

A second objection to IQ tests, whether culture-free or culture-specific, is that they are unable to capture the wide variety of skills that individuals possess. Each person develops a unique combination of talents (in effect, their own mini-culture), and no standardized test can take this kaleidoscopic variety into account. The American linguist William Labov encountered this limitation when attempting to assess the verbal skills of black children from Harlem, in New York. However, when he got to know the children,

LEFT Family influence on the intelligence of an individual wil be felt through both inheritance and upbringing.

RIGHT The cultural limitations inherent in many IQ tests have tended to discriminate against the complex but different linguistic traditions of black Americans.

allowed them to bring a friend along, and sat down on the floor to talk to them, they were revealed to be sophisticated speakers from a background where verbal skills are highly valued. The IQ test can at best give us a crude indication of an individual's intellectual skills that are held to be of value by a given culture, or particular psychologist. At worst, the IQ test provides a gross distortion of the individual's skills, completely ignoring the complex abilities he has almost certainly developed for other tasks.

Intelligence and lifestyle

Those who believe that intelligence is essentially a biologically inherited capacity often point to the significant correlations found between a child's IQ and that of his parents. How could this correlation come about if intelligence is not inherited? All parents provide unique environments for rearing their children. Normally, the environment will be rich enough for the child to exercise a wide range of skills: verbal, spatial, perceptual, motor, etc. At the same time, this environment places limits on the child's opportunity for growth. Even an innate skill requires a suitable environment for it to function adequately. To a considerable extent, the constraints on the child's opportunities are associated with the parent – the parent's job, the family's economic position, the degree to which they play with the child, the parent's attitude as to what is important in child development. All these are crucial social factors in determining the development of the child's intellectual skills. Furthermore, these social determinants have been acquired by the parents themselves during the course of their own development. Many studies point to reproduction of lifestyles within families from one generation to the next, even to the extent that father and son are often found in similar types of employment. It is small wonder that children and their parents tend to fare comparably when asked to perform an IQ test. Their attitudes and opportunities for the development of skills are likely to be very similar.

Types of intelligence

In IQ tests, the measurement of intelligence is evaluated by monitoring performance of a variety of tasks. The most important of these include spatial skills, verbal ability, numerical reasoning, perceptual analysis, and memory. The overall measure of an individual's intelligence reflects his or her achievement across the board. Often psychologists make an assessment of a general measure of intelligence (or "g-factor") underlying performance of the various tests, and report specific results separately.

Human vs. artificial intelligence

As I sit here at my computer I make frequent typing errors, which my word processor often automatically corrects for me. Should this be regarded as intelligent behavior, even though it is completely deterministic, driven by a computer program?

Many commentators would argue that the relatively simple procedures needed for a "spellcheck" do not compare with what is involved in human intelligence. How complicated does the computer's behavior need to be before we attribute it with an artificial intelligence? Today's supercomputers are capable of extremely complex tasks. Their powers of calculation are much greater than ours; they can beat the world champion at chess; small hand-held devices are capable of recognizing their owner's speech; they can navigate space-ships; and they can recognize fingerprints.

Yet most of us would be loath to equate artificial intelligence with human intelligence. One reason for this is that although today's machines may be good at what they do, that is all they are good at: they lack the capacity to coordinate multiple artificial intelligences in new and creative ways. Of course, as we progress further in our understanding of how humans coordinate their intelligences to solve difficult problems, it is likely that we will be able to exploit this knowledge to build truly intelligent machines.

ABOVE AND RIGHT Even as computers become ever more sophisticated, they still cannot perform many disparate tasks simultaneously, something we do all the time.

MULTIPLE INTELLIGENCES

SOME PSYCHOLOGISTS ARGUE that there is more than one type of intelligence. For example, Howard Gardner has proposed a theory of "multiple intelligences," suggesting that intelligence is composed of discrete modules. Each module deals with specific but different kinds of information that individuals encounter in the course of their regular activities. Among these different modules, Gardner includes linguistic intelligence, musical intelligence, logico-mathematical intelligence, spatial intelligence, bodily kinesthetic intelligence, and personal intelligences (access to personal feelings, relations with others, etc.). He suggests that these intelligence modules are genetically preprogrammed, though subject to cultural specialization and educational assistance. Evidence regarding the functional specialization of the brain would seem to support this theory of multiple intelligences. Furthermore, brain damage can lead to selective impairment of particular skills, and there are plenty of people who display exceptional abilities in only one field.

BODILY KINESTHETIC

LINGUISTIC

PERSONAL

INTELLIGENCE

MUSICAL

SPATIAL

LOGICO-MATHEMATICAL

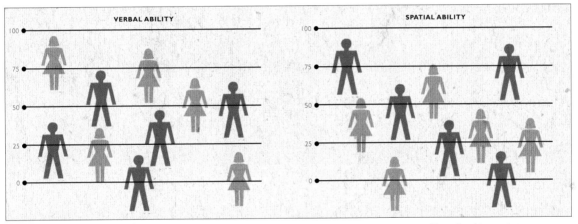

VERBAL ABILITY

SPATIAL ABILITY

Verbal intelligence

Tests of verbal intelligence may involve assessing how quickly an individual can name a picture or solve verbal reasoning problems like "Seed is to plant as egg is to (a) tree, (b) root, (c) pollen, (d) oats, or (e) bird?" Tests of numerical abilities include assessment of how quickly and accurately an individual can perform mental arithmetic or solve numerical reasoning problems – for example, identifying a number omitted from a series.

People often show considerable variation in performance levels across different tests. Some of this variation may be predictable, since women tend to have higher verbal IQ than men, while men tend to have higher spatial IQ than women. However, it should be stressed that the variation in performance normally found within any group is much larger than the small difference in averages between the sexes.

ABOVE There is evidence that women score more highly than men at particular tasks, and vice versa; but the difference in average ability between the sexes is less significant than the overall difference between the highest and lowest scores.

TOP Psychologists argue that "intelligence" is a composite of many different qualities, abilities, and attributes.

Creativity

T*he ability to create is frequently held up as the fundamental quality that distinguishes humans from other animals. Creativity is a talent that everyone shares to some extent, although the activities that we acclaim as "creative" are often very narrowly defined according to our specific cultural prejudices.*

The most obvious examples of human creativity are to be found in the realm of science and the arts. When we think of creative individuals, we think of people who create new objects or ideas, or situate existing objects or ideas in a novel context. Artists and scientists often find it difficult to identify the source of their creativity. The philosopher Karl Popper, for example, had very precise ideas about to how to judge the value of scientific hypotheses – but when it came to explaining their derivation he was hopelessly vague. One sculptor may see an angel coming "out of the stone," while another perceives a wolf in the same piece of rock. Poets and writers have attributed their inspiration to dreams, visions, even pacts with the Devil!

Most of us are creative every time we open our mouths. The American linguist Noam Chomsky pointed out that most of the things we say have never been uttered before. Consider the sentences on this page. I can guarantee that you won't find another page with exactly the same sequence of words in any other book ever written. I offer this guarantee not in testimony of my own creativity, but as an example of what we all routinely accomplish when we speak or write: the creation of novel expressions. Chomsky attributed this creative talent for language to our mastery of a system of grammatical rules. These rules govern how words can be put together to make up sentences. We rarely break these rules, even though we may not be aware of them.

It may seem strange to argue that creativity emerges from obeying rules. However, it was Chomsky's great insight to realize that grammar provides the foundations or framework that allows us to build new expressions. All artists and scientists need tools in order to express their creativity, and we all use grammar as a tool for creative expression.

ABOVE Beginning to see the light… a new understanding, a revelation, a creative notion: the satisfaction of a mind at work.

ALTERED PERCEPTIONS

EVEN SIMPLE ACTS of perception involve creativity. Look at the line drawing reproduced here, known as a Necker Cube. If you stare at it long enough, you will discover that its orientation shifts spontaneously: what was the front face suddenly moves to the rear. The shift results from your own creative perceptual reorganization of the sensory stimulation of your retina. You can't create just any interpretation of the line drawing: your interpretation conforms to your experience of two-dimensional representations of three-dimensional objects. Your own internal knowledge base is at work here.

Given that you know how objects can be represented on a page, artists are able to exploit your creativity to produce representations of ambiguous figures. The surreal paintings of Salvador Dalí, such as "The Metamorphosis of Narcissus," depend on our ability to see two, or sometimes even three, things at once as kneeling figures become faces and waterfalls turn to flowing hair.

NECKER CUBE

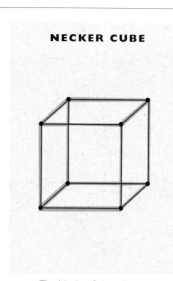

ABOVE The Necker Cube offers a simple challenge to the mind's perceptual adaptability: if you look long enough the front face suddenly moves to the rear.

Cultural criteria

The creative brain achieves novel results by combining well-known building blocks (such as words) in new ways. We all do this continuously in the course of our everyday activities without even thinking about it. But what marks out creativity in cultural terms? Why are some creative acts regarded more highly than others? After all, we don't get excited every time someone utters a sentence never heard before; we probably don't even notice that it has happened. What people regard as creative and value as art varies enormously. You only have to consider the controversy that is provoked when avant-garde works of art are unveiled in international galleries.

What is regarded as creative also varies according to context and fashion. The glass pyramid that provides a spectacular entrance to the Louvre Museum was hailed as a work of genius when it was erected in the 1980s, but probably wouldn't have been regarded as such in ancient Egypt. Nevertheless, the source of all creativity, whether recognized or not, is probably our ability to combine familiar objects and ideas in novel ways – a capacity demonstrated from infancy. Why at a particular point in time an individual comes up with a specific novel combination that is valued by the prevailing culture remains a mystery. At this stage in our understanding, it is more appropriate to ask how rather than why.

BELOW The Louvre pyramid in Paris, designed by I.M. Pei, revisits an ancient architectural style while adding a distinctive modern twist.

Problems

Damage to the brain, as a result of head injury, stroke, or disease, can lead to a wide variety of intellectual, emotional, and motor control problems. The nature of the problem depends on the location of the damage. Some brain lesions produce very noticeable effects, such as complete inability to recognize people. Others lead to much more subtle effects, such as surface dyslexia (see pages 54–5). The consequences of brain damage are often complicated, because brain lesions do not respect the natural lines of organization of the brain and so can have unpredictable effects on behavior. For this reason, the specific pattern that arises tends to be unique to the individual involved.

There are also a variety of problems affecting mental processes that can arise even in the absence of postnatal brain damage or trauma – among them, autism, Asperger's syndrome (a variety of autism where the suffer has normal IQ), Down's syndrome, and Specific Language Impairment. As far as we know, these conditions are genetically determined, though why the genetic abnormality leads to the mental deficiency is not understood.

Autism

For some conditions, such as autism, it is often possible to identify abnormalities of the brain, such as irregularities in the structure of the cerebellum, hippocampus, or limbic system. However, this does not necessarily tell us exactly what the cause of the problem is. Autistic children show normal patterns of development during their early years, but then their linguistic and social development seems to slow down or even stop. They also engage in self-occupied, repetitive movements. Most autistic children have an IQ below the normal range, though some exhibit exceptional skills. For example, there is a very well-

DOWN'S SYNDROME results from a genetic abnormality whereby some of the cells that develop after conception have too many chromosomes. Children with Down's syndrome suffer from heart disease and poor motor control and from severe mental retardation, although, unlike autistic children, sufferers are frequently sociable and outgoing. Although some Down's sufferers live to adulthood, the majority die as children as a result of heart disease. Researchers have been able to identify the genetic abnormalities that give rise to Down's syndrome, but the mechanisms whereby the genetic abnormality leads to the brain dysfunctions still is not known.

ABOVE Mental dysfunctions can arise from abnormalities in the initial construction of the brain as well as from postnatal injury of some kind.

BELOW Motor problems associated with brain injuries can often be alleviated through physiotherapy.

documented case of a severely autistic child, named Nadia, who demonstrated a superb drawing talent. In later years, the repetitive movements tend to disappear, but intellectual and linguistic skills remain below the normal range.

Finding the location

Specific Language Impairment *(see pages 54–5)* is one condition for which it has not been possible to identify obvious abnormalities in the brain. Failure to uncover damage in the brain areas that might be responsible for these types of dysfunction makes it difficult to evaluate hypotheses about their causes. However, new techniques of brain imaging may help us to understand the nature of such problems better. If normal patterns of neurological activity can be mapped, there is more chance of identifying where and why an abnormal pattern occurs.

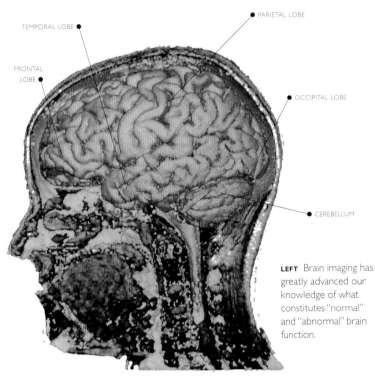

TEMPORAL LOBE

PARIETAL LOBE

FRONTAL LOBE

OCCIPITAL LOBE

CEREBELLUM

LEFT Brain imaging has greatly advanced our knowledge of what constitutes "normal" and "abnormal" brain function.

Brain tumors

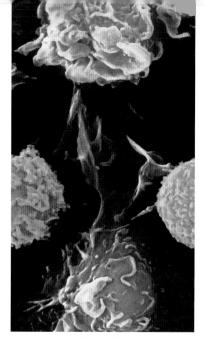

ABOVE Electron micrograph of two cancer cells (colored blue) that have just divided. The pink cells are lymphocytes, part of the body's immune system.

T*umors can develop in any part of the body, and the brain is no exception. The cells of the body are constantly dying off and being replaced by new cells, which are formed by older cells dividing before dying. Tumors occur when this process of cell division gets out of control, and a particular group of cells starts replicating itself and failing to die.*

BELOW The electrical messages that the brain sends out can be detected using electrodes attached to the skull, and a picture of the pattern of activity can be drawn up.

Tumors can originate in the brain itself, or spread to it from the structures adjacent to the brain or from a tumor growing elsewhere in the body. Tumors originating in the brain itself arise from the glial cells and rarely, if ever, from the neurons, which are not replaced after birth. If a tumor grows quickly and invades the neighboring tissues of the body, the tumor is called a cancer. Tumors originating from the glial cells are called gliomas and are often cancerous.

Tumors can also grow from the membrane, called the meninges, that covers the brain. These are called meningiomas and are usually not cancerous. Rather than growing into the brain, they exert pressure on it, often distorting and denting it. Neuromas – tumors that grow from the nerves next to the brain – can have a similar effect.

Gliomas, meningiomas, and neuromas are much rarer in humans than cancers of the prostate, breast, or bowel, and nobody is certain as to precisely why they occur. However, the more common cancers often spread from the original site to the brain, as secondary tumors. In contrast, tumors that originate in the brain never spread to other parts of the body.

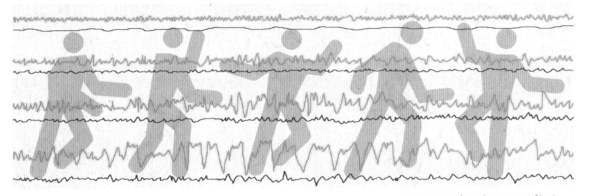

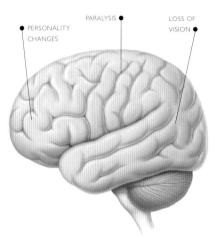

ABOVE EEGs show the pattern of brain activity during sleep, from rapid irregular waves as the subject falls asleep (top) to larger slower oscillations during deepest sleep (bottom).

Symptoms

Brain tumors produce three sorts of symptoms – epilepsy, loss of function of the part of the brain where the tumor is growing, and headaches and vomiting. But there is considerable variation as to which of these symptoms will develop. The pattern of symptoms depends on where the tumor is growing and how quickly. If a slow-growing benign (i.e. non-cancerous) tumor is growing in one of the frontal lobes, it can become very large before it causes any symptoms at all. If a malignant (i.e. cancerous) tumor is growing in the speech area or motor area, it is likely to cause symptoms very quickly, while it is still small.

Generally, tumors at the front of the brain tend to cause personality and intellectual changes; those in the central part of the brain produce progressive paralysis on the opposite side of the body; and ones at the back of the brain cause loss of vision and coordination. Typically, with a tumor these problems become gradually worse, whereas with a stroke the loss of brain function is sudden, and subsequently often improves over time.

PERSONALITY CHANGES

PARALYSIS

LOSS OF VISION

ABOVE The symptoms caused by brain tumors vary according to their position and whether they are cancerous or not.

EEG AS A DIAGNOSTIC TOOL

IF ELECTRODES are attached to the scalp, the electrical activity of the brain can be detected through the skull. These signals are used to produce a record of "brain waves" called an electroencephalogram, or EEG. If your brain is at rest and you have your eyes shut, but are not actually asleep, the main rhythms are alpha waves, which have frequencies of about 10Hz. When you fall asleep, slower rhythms – theta waves (4 to 7Hz) and delta waves (0.5 to 4Hz) – emerge as sleep gets deeper. Much smaller rhythms – beta waves (13 to 30Hz) – replace the alpha rhythms during alertness. Gamma waves (30 to 80Hz) are thought to help synchronize different processing areas and link or "bind" them together when they are analyzing the same object.

Damage to the cerebral cortex causes the waves to become slower and larger, which is useful diagnostically. Epilepsy is the most common neurological disease, occurring in about 0.5 percent of the population. Although it is mainly diagnosed from its very characteristic symptoms, an EEG is often used to corroborate the diagnosis.

Psychosurgery

*B*rain surgery is usually thought of as a profession requiring enormous skill and dexterity, although the history of the practice might bring this into question. Crude invasive surgery was used to treat all kinds of disorders from depression to schizophrenia. Although such practices have long been rejected, more precise methods of psychosurgery, backed up by the insights gained from brain imaging, are now being considered as a response to disorders such as Parkinson's disease.

Until thirty or forty years ago, "psychosurgery" – deliberately destroying part of the brain in order to treat mental illness – was widely used. Experimental work in animals had shown that operations to disconnect the frontal lobes from the rest of the brain could make the animals docile. The operation was called a lobectomy or lobotomy. In the 1930s a Portuguese neurosurgeon, António Egas Moniz, suggested that a similar operation might be beneficial for people suffering from severe mental illness, and he carried out such work until he was shot by one of his patients and left paralyzed. In 1949 he was awarded a Nobel prize for his contribution to our understanding of the physiology of medicine. Over the next twenty years, many thousands of psychiatric patients underwent psychosurgical operations, all over the world. At first, these were very extensive, involving the entire separation of the frontal lobes from the rest of the brain. In later operations the area of brain destroyed was reduced, and the indications for surgery became more specific. These operations are now only rarely practiced and have fallen into disrepute.

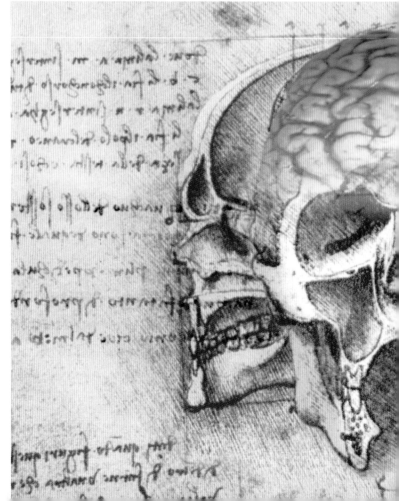

BELOW From the Middle Ages to the present, the methods that have been used to find out what goes on "inside the head" have reflected the attitudes to the brain that prevailed at the time.

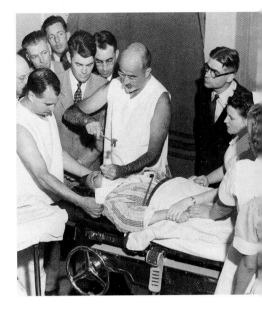

THE DANGERS OF REDUCTIONISM

EACH AGE SEEKS to understand the brain by reference to the latest technology and scientific discoveries. Psychosurgery reflected the growing understanding in the early decades of the twentieth century about how the main organ systems of the body, such as the heart and lungs, and liver, work. And since the brain was regarded as an "organ," it followed that its lobes had identifiable "functions." This is, of course, true to an extent, but the important point is the immense complexity of the brain when compared to the other organ systems of the body.

The advocates of psychosurgery were eminent and respected doctors; they thought they were at the forefront of medical science and wrote learned treatises about the merits of psychosurgery. And yet they have now become objects of contempt, and their books make painful reading. Today, in the age of the digital computer, when trying to explain the brain, many people characterize it as a computer. Research may show that our brains are indeed like computers, but the era of psychosurgery should remind us of the dangers of reductionism when trying to understand the human brain.

RIGHT Although gruesome and crude, surgery was the only option available to sufferers from mental illness before drug therapy was developed.

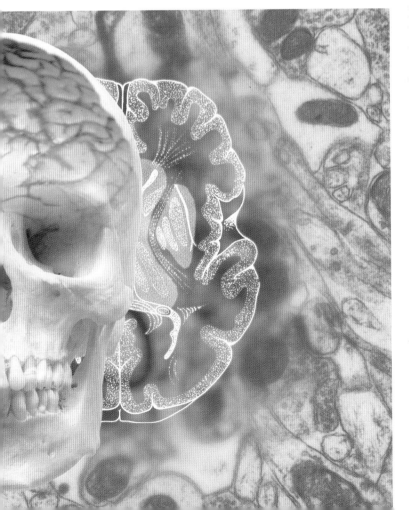

From our present viewpoint, it is easy to dismiss the lobotomies performed during the first half of the twentieth century as crude, and even barbaric. It must be remembered, however, that before the advent of modern drug therapy, little could be done for patients suffering from severe psychiatric illness other than to lock them away in mental hospitals. In retrospect it seems that some patients – especially those with "obsessional–compulsive" disorders – were actually helped by surgical treatment of this sort, particularly when the operation involved very small and precise targets in the brain. Nevertheless, many other patients – probably the majority – were left apathetic and dependent by their surgery, and suffered catastrophic personality changes.

The size and complexity of the frontal lobes of our brain distinguishes us from other animals. But, while there is unanimous agreement that the function of the heart is to pump blood around the body, we cannot ascribe any straightforward function to the frontal lobes of the human brain – other than that they makes us characteristically ourselves and generically different from the family pet!

Schizophrenia

*S*chizophrenia is a term that was introduced around the beginning of the twentieth century. Most people think that it means having a "split personality," but that isn't really right. It is better thought of as a disorder of thinking and feeling. The "split" relates to components of thoughts that wouldn't normally be separated – so mere fragments of ideas and concepts may be associated together, seemingly without logic or reason. In this way, sufferers can form ideas and beliefs that normal people regard as bizarre and utterly unpredictable.

DEFINITIONS

There is some debate as to whether schizophrenia is really so very different from other psychiatric conditions. Patients in the manic phase of manic depression may hear voices, see things that aren't really there, and entertain deluded notions, in much the same way that schizophrenic patients do. What leads to the eventual diagnosis and treatment often depends on the overall pattern of abnormal behavior in the longer term.

Schizophrenia tends to strike relatively early in adult life. Sufferers and their families can thus face many years of coping with the condition. Although a minority of patients may have a single episode from which they recover permanently, others have recurrent episodes, each requiring admission to hospital, or may become permanently resident in a mental hospital. In this respect, schizophrenia is quite unlike senile dementias, such as Alzheimer's disease. Since these are predominately diseases of old age, they do not prevent sufferers from spending most of their life happily and productively. Sadly, schizophrenia often does just that.

Basic characteristics

People have disagreed about the diagnosis of schizophrenia ever since the term was first introduced by a Swiss psychiatrist, Eugen Bleuler (the term is Greek for "split mind"). One major issue is whether it lumps together patients who don't in fact share a common condition. Individual patients can have quite different symptoms, different disease courses, and different responses to the drugs used to treat them. The original classification of what are now called the schizophrenias was based on two major features. First, they were conditions that typically began at a relatively early age; second, and crucially, they had a poor prognosis. Sufferers were described as tending to get progressively worse, or at least as

suffering from frequent relapses. Although modern classification focuses on particular patterns of disordered thought, it still retains the idea that the condition must be more than just a single short-lived episode.

Diagnosis and prediction

Gradually psychiatrists have come to agree on the key points that identify schizophrenia. Nowadays the most widely accepted method of diagnosis is based on the diagnostic and statistical manual (generally shortened to DSM) of the American Psychiatric Association, which is used to assess disturbances of thinking, feeling, and social behavior. But even when all of these are disturbed, a diagnosis of schizophrenia is not made until symptoms have been present for at least six months. In this sense, schizophrenia is still thought of as a lasting condition. One reason for this is that people who experience brief schizophrenialike episodes tend to have a better prognosis.

As yet there is no reliable way to predict whether or not a particular child will develop schizophrenia. Although recent studies demonstrate that schizophrenics have tended to show abnormal behavior patterns while still children, these are not very strong correlations. Schizophrenia most probably results from a combination of genetic and environmental factors, each contributing to the chance that we will or will not develop the condition. So we might have a genetic makeup that predisposes us to develop the condition, but never encounter an environment that causes the tendency to be expressed. Or we might be genetically fortunate enough to have a low predisposition, but unlucky enough to meet an environmental challenge severe enough to trigger schizophrenia. It seems that until the causes are clearer, we may have to think in terms such as these.

ABOVE Schizophrenia, though a controversial disorder, is believed to involve a lack of coordination between thinking and feeling aspects of the personality.

LEFT Schizophrenia shares a number of similarities with other psychiatric conditions: its defining characteristic is its persistence.

RIGHT Many people may have a genetic predisposition to schizophrenia, but never encounter the circumstances which might trigger it. It's like the toss of a coin.

Schizophrenia
Symptoms and treatment

BELOW The symptoms of schizophrenia are often divided into two groups: positive (things schizophrenics do that other people don't) and negative (things schizophrenics don't do that most people do).

Throughout most of human history, schizophrenia has been untreatable, partly because no one understood the sources and reasons for the symptoms. Schizophrenia plausibly underlies some accounts of demonic possession and witchcraft. Experiencing schizophrenia is bad enough, and who knows what dreadful additional tortures sufferers may have undergone as a result of their contemporaries' misguided attempts to treat the condition or punish them for their abnormal behavior? During the second half of the twentieth century, we have made some progress in developing effective treatments. In the process we have gathered clues about what is going wrong in schizophrenics' brains, and these should in turn help us to refine and improve treatment.

ABOVE Schizophrenia might have been behind the behavior of people who, in the past, were reviled as witches.

Symptoms

The symptoms of schizophrenia are many and varied. So is there just one condition, with a single cause, a single prognosis, and a single relevant treatment? Or is there, in reality, a collection of different conditions? One way to approach this has been to divide the symptoms into two groups. The first group (the "positive symptoms") is made up of things that schizophrenics do, but normal people don't – like hearing voices, or believing that their thoughts have been inserted into their minds by some outside force. The second group (the "negative symptoms") is made up of things like a lack of social and emotional responsiveness – aspects of behavior that most people have, but schizophrenics do not. It is possible for the same person to show both positive and negative symptoms. So are these groups really different? The answer is probably "yes" – in fact, the latest thinking suggests there should be three groups of symptoms, rather than two.

Treatment

Until the 1950s, treatment for schizophrenia concentrated on protecting the patients from themselves, and protecting society at large from the patients by keeping them in institutions. Current medicine didn't have much to offer beyond confinement and restraint. Patients in mental asylums were sometimes forcibly restrained in cold baths – which seemed to have a temporary calming effect – but there were no treatments that acted to restore normal thought.

Then a French psychiatrist decided to try a new drug, which had recently been introduced to calm patients before surgery, to see if it would help calm his psychiatric patients, too. The results were astonishing. The drug did indeed calm the patients. And, given time, it also seemed to restore more normal thinking patterns. The hallucinations and delusions ceased. Suddenly it was possible to treat the patients' abnormal thinking, rather than just coping with its consequences.

But unfortunately the drugs developed for the treatment of schizophrenia deal with the positive symptoms more effectively than the negative symptoms. So these miraculous antipsychotic drugs have their limitations, and they also have their costs. The key antipsychotic effect comes from blocking the action of a particular brain chemical, the neurotransmitter dopamine. But dopamine is essential for normal movement (Parkinson's disease is caused by a loss of one group of dopamine cells in the brain). In addition, it is involved in the experience of pleasure. Natural pleasures such as sex lead to dopamine release. So do the synthetic pleasures of drugs such as cocaine and amphetamines; indeed, amphetamine abuse can lead to a schizophrenialike mental disorder. Blocking dopamine certainly reduces some of the symptoms of schizophrenia, but at the same time it may cause movement disorders and reduce the intensity of pleasures. So these drugs are not an unmixed blessing, and patients often abandon treatment because of unpleasant side effects.

The development of drugs with fewer side effects has therefore become a priority in the field of schizophrenia research. Some of the newer "atypical" antipsychotics produce less movement disorder than the older treatments, though having other side effects of their own; and some of them seem to help with negative symptoms, too.

BELOW Schizophrenia affects perhaps one in a hundred people, causing considerable suffering and sometimes drastic repercussions.

Schizophrenia
What are the causes?

ABOVE Studies of identical twins show that if one twin is schizophrenic, the other is very likely to develop schizophrenia as well, suggesting that a genetic factor governs predisposition to schizophrenia.

Schizophrenia is thought to involve an alteration in function of the temporal lobes and the amygdala, the regions that comprise the limbic system. The fact that the symptoms often appear at an early age, from adolescence onward, suggests that it is caused by a developmental abnormality of this area rather than a degeneration of healthy tissue – an abnormality that has its roots in a genetic defect. This theory is supported by clear evidence of a strong genetic factor that increases the probability of developing schizophrenia. Within the population as a whole, the chances of developing schizophrenia are one in a hundred; but if you have a schizophrenic brother or sister, the chances rises to one in fifty, or to one in ten if he or she is your identical twin. It has also been shown that schizophrenia tends to strike males at an earlier age than females. And there may be environmental factors, since the incidence of schizophrenic births goes up following flu epidemics.

As yet there is no incontrovertible proof that schizophrenia is associated with biochemical changes in the limbic system, although the likelihood that a modification of the dopamine system may be involved is extremely strong. Imaging studies have revealed a shrinkage of this area, and it may be that further imaging studies will provide conclusive evidence.

Chemical clues

Much of what we know about schizophrenia has been deduced from the nature of the drugs that reduce the symptoms. Antischizophrenic drugs, or neuroleptics (literally, "neuron-claspers"), were accidentally discovered in the 1950s when it was found that chlorpromazine could control the positive symptoms of schizophrenia. Chlorpromazine and other neuroleptics work against the action of certain dopamine receptors, called D2 receptors. These receptors are inhibitory, and occur in the corpus striatum, the hypothalamus, and the limbic system: the target regions of the three major dopamine pathways in the central nervous system. So the dopamine system would appear to be central to the problem.

THE MAIN DOPAMINE PATHWAYS

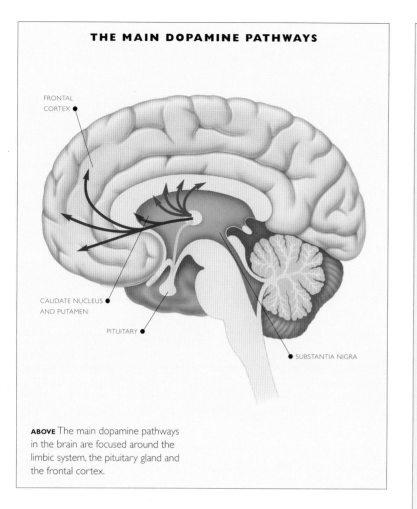

FRONTAL CORTEX

CAUDATE NUCLEUS AND PUTAMEN

PITUITARY

SUBSTANTIA NIGRA

ABOVE The main dopamine pathways in the brain are focused around the limbic system, the pituitary gland and the frontal cortex.

NEW DRUGS

The likelihood, suggested by evidence from brain imaging, that schizophrenia is associated with abnormalities in various regions of the brain cortex may well lead to the development of more appropriate drugs. Hallucinations and delusions are associated with changes in the temporal lobes; social withdrawal and slowed thinking with changes in the frontal lobes; and confusion with changes in the cingulate cortex. It's possible that some of these cortical changes in turn produce the changes in the dopamine system that current drug treatments aim to reverse. A possible strategy could therefore be to develop new drugs that would target these primary cortical changes. We might then be able to get away from dopamine "blockade" and its problematic side effects.

Other factors

Further evidence for the involvement of the limbic dopamine system is that amphetamine – a drug that causes an excessive release of dopamine in the brain *(see pages 94–5)* – induces a state of psychosis that is not unlike the positive symptoms of schizophrenia. Furthermore, postmortem examinations of tissue from schizophrenic patients have revealed an increase in the number of D2 dopamine receptors. However, this evidence needs to be treated with caution, because prolonged exposure to a cocktail of therapeutic drugs during the lifetime of a schizophrenic patient could produce the same effect.

It has also been suggested that 5-hydroxytryptamine (5-HT) deficiency might cause schizophrenia. This idea is based on the fact that drugs such as LSD, which act on the 5-HT receptors, can induce hallucinations. At present, there is little further evidence for this theory. As with most disorders of the central nervous system, the underlying causes of schizophrenia are poorly understood. While the neuroleptics effectively treat the positive symptoms, they do nothing to reverse the root cause, and relapse occurs if treatment ceases.

ABOVE Pharmacological research may hold the key to developing a more effective treatment, or even a cure, for schizophrenia.

chapter five
the aging brain

As far as the brain is concerned, aging is
not simply a process of decay, but is also the
culmination of a process of memory gathering
that has continued since birth, and that
provides us with the wisdom of age.

The Aging Brain
introduction

ABOVE A huge amount of memory, and wisdom, stored under a parasol… The organization of memory is one of the keys to understanding how the brain operates.

Most of us in Western cultures view old age as a time of decay and debilitation. So far as the vital organs of the body, our skin condition, and the strength of our muscles are concerned, this gloomy attitude may be valid – but for the brain, aging is a much more ambiguous process.

As we saw at the start of this book, of all the species on Earth, we humans are closest to the "nurture" end of the nature/nurture spectrum, and our brains are constantly changing as a result of our experiences. Small wonder, then, that memory is one of the key processes that contributes to what makes each of us special. And if memories are continually accumulated throughout life, then old age provides an opportunity for those memories to help us to interpret life – to be wise – more than at any other stage in our existence.

As will become apparent from this chapter, there are basically two approaches to the study of memory. The first is to look at the macro brain, to work at the level of what are termed the gross brain regions. Because we now have a very good idea of what happens to memory when these regions are damaged or stimulated, we are starting to get an overall picture of how memory is organized by the brain. Although there is much still to discover, it is now clear that there is more than one type of memory. For example, in brain terms, the kind of memory required for a skill such as driving is very different from a memory of a special day at the beach with a childhood friend. Moreover, each of these different types of memory process relies on the coordination of more than one region of the brain. But the great question is

RIGHT When memory fades, for instance in cases of Alzheimer's disease, what is actually going wrong in the brain? We don't yet understand the details.

exactly what happens within each brain area. Irrespective of whether memories are stored away like files (which happens not to be the case), there is the riddle that memories endure even though brain cells are constantly being changed and chemicals replaced.

The second approach for the study of memory is at the level of single cells. Although much is now known about how cells can be modified and how they contact neighboring cells in a network, we still do not know how these cellular events at the micro level are translated into the specializations seen in larger brain areas. Nowhere is this more problematic than in trying to pinpoint how and why things go wrong – for example, in Alzheimer's disease, a brain disorder tragically characterized by memory loss. Although the brain regions that are most affected have long been identified, the search is still on to discover the cellular mechanism of destruction. Similarly, with another great scourge of old age, Parkinson's disease, we need to "bridge" the levels – to discover the relationship between micro and macro – in order to understand how the cell death that occurs in a tiny, very specific, part of the brain is translated into the characteristic large-scale poverty of movement.

Perhaps most important of all, it should be borne in mind that, although these degenerative disorders are widespread today, they are not inevitable consequences of old age. Not only will improved understanding of such disorders inspire better therapies for those specifically affected; a healthier and more active lifestyle should mean that more of us can look forward to a clear-minded and able-minded old age.

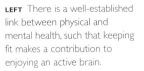

LEFT There is a well-established link between physical and mental health, such that keeping fit makes a contribution to enjoying an active brain.

RIGHT On a psychological level, maintaining a youthful outlook helps to promote a healthy progression into older age, and to keep the brain in good order.

Memory

ABOVE Remembering a telephone number is one example of short-term memory; we only need to retain the information for as long as it takes to dial it.

*W*e have many different memory stores, which allow us to retain and recall a variety of types of information: names, dates, events or scenes from the past, how to perform a particular skill, how to find our way around our hometown. Some stores hold onto information for only a short time; others can store it for much longer.

Short-term memory has a limited capacity. It lets us repeat a string of, say, six or eight words or numbers that we heard or saw a few seconds ago (enabling us to look up a number in the phone book and then dial it), but it can't store the whole of a string twice that length. New information bumps out old; so we tend to remember the last few numbers in a series that's too long for short-term storage, and when we make mistakes in short-term recall, they often sound like the correct answer or bear a close resemblance to it.

Long-term memory stores are quite different. For one thing there seems to be no limit to their capacity. Our mistakes in long-term recall often make some meaningful association, although the facts we give are inaccurate or the details confused. Very short-term memory and distant memory are spared during the early stages of Alzheimer's disease, when day-to-day memory is already failing. Concussion resulting from a blow to the head can, in contrast, erase memory for what happened just beforehand, while again typically sparing memories from the distant past.

LEFT Memories are stored and retrieved in different ways: childhood memories often have great staying power even when much else is gone.

Memory storage at cell level

How do the billions of nerve cells in the brain store our memories? Each nerve cell is connected to a network of many, many others, each helping to control the others' activity. The way particular nerve cells control the activity of the cells they're connected to can be modified as a result of our experiences – thus changing the patterns of nerve-cell activity in our brains.

These changes are crucial for the way memories are laid down. If memories are represented as patterns of activity in networks of nerve cells, then it follows that there is no single place where a particular memory is stored. Instead, it is stored by the activities of many different nerve cells, even though the relevant nerve cells may all be within a particular structure in the brain.

As cells age, they probably lose some of their adaptability. But fortunately this kind of storage system is very flexible. It has huge storage capacity and can still retain information pretty accurately when some of its component nerve cells are damaged. It is also able to retrieve the right answer when given only partial information. Computer memory systems have a long way to go in order to catch up.

ABOVE Memory depends on a complex network of nerve cells, flexible enough to be able to adapt even to partial damage.

BELOW Damage to the memory facility can be severely disabling, particularly in cases where it affects our relationships and our sense of self.

MEMORY DAMAGE

DAMAGE TO THE CEREBRAL CORTEX as a whole impairs memory. In addition, more localized damage to the brain areas that play a key role in laying down memories can lead to serious impairment. In both situations, very short-term memory and remote memories are much less likely to be damaged than day-to-day memory.

An example of the first kind of diffuse memory impairment is Alzheimer's disease, a degenerative process affecting the cortex. Sufferers gradually lose their day-to-day memory, and eventually their remote memory and very short-term memory as well. People suffering from such problems often have well-preserved memories of the distant past – and can often remember how to perform skills such as playing a musical instrument – but cannot take in any new information at all.

An example of more localized damage causing severe impairment is the viral brain infection *herpes encephalitis*. This disease attacks the temporal lobes, and in severe cases the ability to lay down new memories is completely destroyed. They are "lost in time," condemned to live in the present. They have all their past memories intact, so they know who they are and where they are – but they have no idea how they got there and forget everything that happens to them within a few minutes. Everything we do depends on being able to keep a sense of continuity between the past and the present, and severe short-term memory loss of this kind makes it impossible to lead any kind of independent life.

Alzheimer's disease

*A*lzheimer's disease or DAT (dementia of the Alzheimer type), as scientists now call it, is not an inevitable consequence of aging. In fact, it appears to occur as a result of distinct biological changes. And this has inspired an increasing number of research groups to work toward a treatment for a distressing condition that afflicts a great many people every year and ultimately leads to death.

DAT affects roughly four percent of the population in the West, but the true percentage may well be higher, because the only way to make a definitive diagnosis is by performing a biopsy on the tissue after death. A postmortem biopsy reveals two distinct hallmarks of Alzheimer pathology: senile plaques and neurofibrillary tangles. Both are found to some extent in all aged brains, but the levels in Alzheimer brains are very much greater.

Plaques and tangles

Senile plaques (patches of diseased tissue) form outside the cells and consist of a beta-amyloid protein (Aβ) along with aggregates of neuronal and glial tissue. Aβ can be neurotoxic in its own right, but whether plaque formation is a cause or an effect of brain-cell degeneration is not known. Senile plaques are found in many parts of the brain, so it would appear that the tissue does not come from a single class of neuron.

Unlike senile plaques, neurofibrillary tangles occur within the cells. A τ-protein that is normally involved in maintaining the architecture of the cell forms abnormal paired helical filaments. These filaments accumulate as tangles within the cell body, possibly disrupting the functions of the cell. When the cell dies, these tangles accumulate in the spaces between cells, often within the senile plaques.

Although these abnormalities are crucial indicators in the postmortem diagnosis of DAT, at present it is not known what role, if any, either of them plays in its development.

For a long time, DAT was believed to involve a progressive breakdown of the cholinergic input (the supply of the neurotransmitter acetylcholine) from the basal forebrain to the hippocampus and cortex. But while it is true that these cholinergic projections degenerate in DAT, other populations of neurons are also affected. So DAT cannot be caused by the loss of a select group of neurons, as happens with Parkinson's disease. This makes it all the more difficult to understand and treat DAT.

Slow progress

Most therapeutic strategies are aimed primarily at replacing lost acetylcholine, but these are proving less than successful. Current research is therefore focusing on inhibiting the disease process by blocking beta-amyloid formation, and the damage to the τ-protein. However, unless we can discover the underlying cause of the degeneration in DAT, it may prove impossible to develop a strategy for treatment, particularly as replacement therapy – the mainstay of much drug treatment – seems to be impractical, because of the varied nature of the cells that are lost. But both the pharmaceutical industry and national governments have realized the enormous potential benefits of Alzheimer treatment, particularly in view of the increasing population of elderly people. Consequently, research into DAT is now one of the biggest single areas of biomedical research.

LEFT Alzheimer's disease is one of the most distressing afflictions associated with old age, not least because its exact cause remains uncertain.

Movement

How do you control your movements? A reasonable assumption would be that you move your arm toward an object by assessing the separation between the two, then moving your arm to reduce the separation until it reaches the target. This is called negative feedback control, because the arm's position is fed back to the controller and subtracted from the position of the target until the difference is zero._

This is how you would operate a crane, but it's not how you move your arm. Although you use the position of the target to calculate where to move the limb, you can't use the reducing distance between them to guide it, because the feedback is too slow.

Consider soccer. When a soccer player kicks the ball from the penalty spot, it takes only a fifth of a second to reach the back of the net. Yet it takes a quarter of a second to react to a visual stimulus, so the goalkeeper's only chance of stopping the ball is to predict which way it will go and move as the striker kicks it. Such movements need to be preprogrammed in a "feedforward" manner, so they achieve their objectives without waiting for feedback. The basic structure of such a program is determined by the basal ganglia, while the cerebellum sets the parameters.

Running the program

Like the sensory systems, the motor system consists of many parallel pathways, each with slightly different functions. They can be divided into two main systems. The first is concentrated around the midline of the brainstem and in the anterior columns of white matter in the spinal cord. It governs the midline muscles of the neck, trunk, and back and the shoulders and thighs, and so controls posture, limb movement, and walking. The second, which lies on the outside of the brainstem and in the lateral columns of the spinal cord, controls the finger and toe muscles for precision grip and tactile identification.

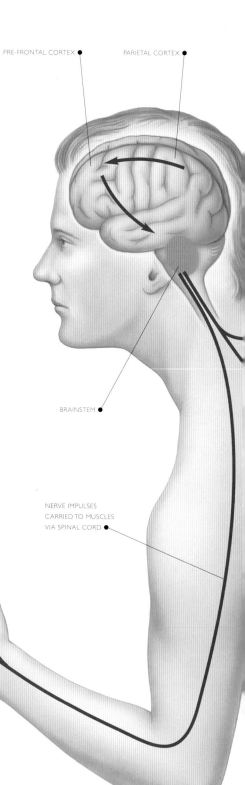

PRE-FRONTAL CORTEX

PARIETAL CORTEX

BRAINSTEM

NERVE IMPULSES
CARRIED TO MUSCLES
VIA SPINAL CORD

ABOVE Movement is in a sense the most important function that our brains carry out for us – without the ability to move, a whole range of human experiences is denied to us.

LEFT All messages to do with movement travel from the motor cortex via the brainstem along pathways in the spinal cord to the relevant muscles.

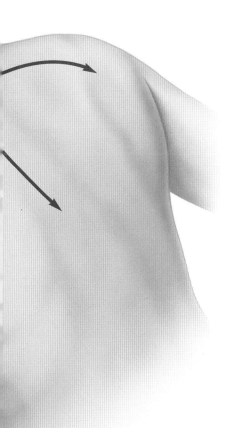

RIGHT The range of movements of which we are capable is enormous, and our hands especially can move with speed, strength, subtlety, and precision as the situation demands.

When movement is controlled visually, signals from the "where" pathway leading from the visual system run to the parietal cortex, which orients attention and limb movements in the appropriate direction. The signals then pass to the prefrontal cortex, which makes the decision to move. They also pass to the basal ganglia – which chooses the basic program for the movement – and to the cerebellum, where the program is calibrated.

The information is then projected back to the relevant areas of the motor cortex, which start executing the program by sending signals to the motor neurons in the spinal cord. The signals then pass down the axons of the motor neurons to the muscles in the limbs, where they trigger the appropriate contractions.

The cerebellum

The cerebellum is a separate organ, joined to the rest of the brain by three bundles of fibers called the cerebellar peduncles. Its function is to set the parameters of any motor program selected by the basal ganglia and generated by the motor cortex, brainstem, and spinal cord, and to calibrate the program so it is precisely tailored to the demands of the moment.

In order for the cerebellum to refine the control system in this way, it needs to be able to predict the outcome of any movement. It does this by receiving inputs from all the motor and sensory systems. Repeated association of a particular motor output with its consequences, in terms of sensory feedback, enables the cerebellum to predict the outcome of a movement and therefore optimize its control.

All this means that the cerebellum plays a vital part in the development of automatic motor skills. It is also employed in the cognitive functions involved in a variety of skilled movements (including speech). As a result, damage to the cerebellum causes lack of coordination, wobbling gait, intention tremor, and shaking hands.

Reflexes and disorders

N‌ot all of our movements are processed via the complex cortical systems described on the previous pages. There is a whole range of movements that we can perform without any conscious control. In fact, we only really become aware of the array of movements we carry out every day if disease damages our motor control system in some way.

Spinal reflexes

The "high-level" motor-control systems are superimposed upon a basic functional organization of reflexes, generated in the spinal cord. Reflexes are automatic stereotyped responses to specific sensory stimuli. They received their name because the ancient Greeks thought that the sensory energy stimulating them was piped by hollow nerve fibers to the spinal cord and from there directly reflected back out to the muscle, causing it to contract. Even if the spinal cord is completely separated from the rest of the brain, as sometimes happens as the result of an accident, it is still able to generate simple reflexes.

Many reflexes play a part in maintaining vital functions such as breathing. The function of other reflexes is less clear, although some are obviously concerned with self-protection. For instance, if a toe is pinched, the leg withdraws very rapidly, as a result of the spinal pain-withdrawal reflex.

ABOVE Our ability to use our bodies — to move, run, stand, reach up, lie down — depends on the complex interaction of our brain and nervous systems.

LEFT The spinal pain-withdrawal reflex acts without our conscious control to protect the body from injury. So if your toe is pinched, your leg will move away quickly from the cause of the pain.

MULTIPLE SCLEROSIS

The nerve fibers of the brain and spinal cord are sheathed with a fatty substance called myelin. This protects the nerve axons and also acts as insulation, allowing electrical impulses to move quickly and uninterruptedly along the nerves. In multiple sclerosis this myelin sheathing degenerates so that the axon is exposed and the flow of electrical impulses is disrupted. This results in loss of sensation, poor balance, and (because the optic nerves are often affected) deterioration in eyesight. Only a relatively limited number of sufferers become completely disabled, but the disease is presently incurable.

When a limb is extended, stretching the flexor muscles, they automatically contract, as if trying to maintain the same length. This is the simplest reflex of all: the length receptors in the muscle sense the stretching and feed this information to the motor neurons in the spinal cord that supply that muscle, triggering the reflex contraction. Even this simple reflex requires the inhibition of the antagonistic muscles on the other side of the joint. This is the function of inhibitory interneurons, which are messengers that translate the initial contraction into reciprocal antagonist inhibition.

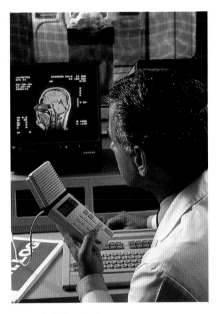

ABOVE Brain imaging is one means of establishing how disorders of movement arise and hence how they might be treated.

HUNTINGTON'S CHOREA

THE HEREDITARY GENETIC DISEASE Huntington's chorea gets its name from the Greek word for dance, *chorea*, because the patients' involuntary movements make it appear as though they are continually dancing. The initial movement disorder is caused by degeneration of inhibitory neurons in one of the four basal ganglia nuclei, the caudate nucleus, which results in a loss of motor control and produces the unwanted dancelike movements. In the later stages of the disease the cerebral cortex degenerates as well, and sufferers become completely demented.

Although fortunately rare, Huntington's chorea is a peculiarly sinister disease because the mutation in the Huntington gene is dominant and therefore very likely to be passed onto the patient's children. However, the first symptoms of the disease do not emerge until middle age, by which time the sufferer would probably have already had children and therefore passed on the disease. Nowadays, if Huntington's chorea is known to be in a family, it is possible to test for the disease before the symptoms emerge, so a decision not to have children can be made. But of course the test also reveals whether the potential sufferer has to face the prospect of this horrible, and ultimately fatal, disease.

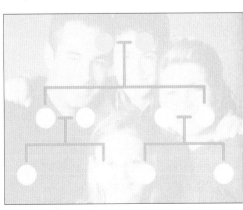

RIGHT Embryonic screening for genetic abnormalities is increasingly common, and some disorders can be treated if detected, but the only way to prevent Huntington's chorea from being passed on is not to have children at all.

Parkinson's disease

Parkinson's disease is a motor-control disorder that causes difficulty in movement initiation and slowness in execution of movement, as well as distressing involuntary movements such as tremor, shaking, and dancing or throwing actions. Each of these involuntary movements is a complete and roughly coordinated motor program in itself, but it is released again and again, totally inappropriately, making normal life difficult or impossible.

ABOVE Suffering repeated blows to the head, as a result for instance of a career as a soccer player, has been identified as one possible cause of Parkinson's disease.

Buried in the middle of each cerebral hemisphere lie four nuclei called the basal ganglia. These are connected to a dark-pigmented nucleus in the brainstem known as the substantia nigra (Latin for "black substance"). The function of the basal ganglia is to select, from a store of prototype motor programs in the cerebral cortex and brainstem, the program most suitable for whatever movement task you are trying to perform. Many of the connections are inhibitory, restraining the program generators in the motor cortex and brainstem, so any damage to the basal ganglia or the substantia nigra not only prevents the selection of movements that a person wants to make, but may also result in the activation of programs that are not wanted. This condition is known as Parkinson's disease.

Like many other afflictions, Parkinson's disease does not have a single root cause. Trauma (Parkinson's disease often develops in boxers and soccer players, who receive numerous blows to the head), certain toxins, viral infections, and neuroleptic drugs (such as those used to treat schizophrenia) can all produce Parkinsonlike effects. But the single largest root cause of the degeneration that leads to Parkinsonism is unknown (or, in medical language, "idiopathic").

Dopamine

Degeneration of the substantia nigra results in Parkinson's disease because the nucleus produces the neurotransmitter dopamine, which helps to select appropriate motor programs. The progressive loss of the dopamine neurons disrupts the balance of two parallel pathways, causing an increase in the inhibitory pathway. However, the symptoms do not emerge until as many as 80 percent of the dopamine neurons are lost, which implies a strong compensatory mechanism. Apparently, the surviving dopamine neurons increase production, while the postsynaptic neurons develop more dopamine receptors. There is also evidence that the uptake of the released dopamine is decreased, so it lasts longer and has greater scope for action.

TREATING THE SYMPTOMS

SINCE THE SYMPTOMS of Parkinson's disease arise from lack of dopamine, they can be alleviated – initially at least – by drugs that either increase dopamine levels or mimic its effects. But although effective in the short term, this strategy does nothing to halt the progressive neuronal loss which, when complete, is fatal.

Two controversial alternative strategies have been attempted. First, transplants of fetal tissue to replace the dopamine neurons have been tried, with some success. Second, lesions of other regions in the brain – notably the globus pallidus and the thalamus – have been employed in an attempt to redress the balance between the direct and indirect pathways. In the future, these techniques may prove more effective than current pharmaceutical therapy. However, they still treat the symptoms rather than the cause, so they are unlikely to be effective in halting the progress of the disease.

FAMOUS SUFFERERS

The uncertainty surrounding the causes of Parkinson's disease is reflected in the variety of types of people who are afflicted by this disorder. Well-known sufferers include Pope John Paul II, the actor Michael J. Fox, and perhaps most famously, the world champion boxer Muhammad Ali. The cases of the Pope and the boxer conform with two of the suggested causes (the aging process and head injuries), but there is no obvious reason why Michael J. Fox, who was in his thirties when the disease was diagnosed, should have been struck down.

RIGHT Well-known sufferers from Parkinson's disease have helped to increase public awareness, and in some cases have raised funds to help fight the disease.

LEFT Parkinson's disease is unusual in that it can be linked to a very specific area of the brain, increasing the chances that a successful treatment will be found.

MICHAEL J. FOX

MUHAMMAD ALI

POPE JOHN PAUL II

Recovery from strokes

ABOVE A picked apple will never recover from bruising, but a living, growing plant finds ways of coping with limited amounts of damage. In the same way, the brain, like other parts of the body, has mechanisms for mending itself.

Many people think that all brain damage is irreversible – but the brain has, in fact, great capacity for recovering from injury. The most common cause of injury to the brain in modern life is a stroke. This occurs either as a result of a blood clot or when a blood vessel supplying the brain becomes blocked off, causing an "infarct" or death of tissue (see pages 54–5). The second most common source of brain damage is from traumatic head injuries. Very little is understood about exactly how the brain recovers from injury, but some general observations can be made.

The younger the patient, the better the chances of recovery. Indeed, it is recognized that in children under one year of age the brain can, in effect, "reprogram" itself. For example, as we have already seen, if the area of the left hemisphere normally responsible for language development is damaged early in life, then speech will develop in the right hemisphere instead. This plasticity, the capacity of the brain to "reshape" itself, is lost as we grow older.

Factors that affect recovery

Some areas of the brain are more vulnerable than others. A small lesion in the brainstem can cause severe disability, whereas a lesion of the same size elsewhere (for instance, in the right frontal lobe) may cause no detectable problems at all. Brain surgeons therefore talk of "eloquent" and "silent" areas of the brain.

HELPING RECOVERY

It is well established that people who have suffered a stroke make a better recovery if they receive intensive physiotherapy and rehabilitation than if they do not. This is in accord with what we have already seen of the brain's ability to develop and recreate itself given the appropriate stimulation. The actual mechanisms of recovery, however, are not known.

Sadly, with severe strokes, matter ultimately triumphs over mind, as there is a limit to how far anyone can recover from extensive brain damage.

LEFT Replacing the dominoes – and rebuilding the brain's processing capabilities through targeted exercises.

ABOVE Brain damage following physical injury is not necessarily all immediate, but may follow the pattern of a progressive domino effect. Brain researchers are investigating whether the process can be interrupted, which would minimize the damage.

DAMAGE LIMITATION

RECENT RESEARCH SUGGESTS that when damage occurs to brain cells a progressive series of chemical reactions is triggered in the cells. This means that the damage does not all occur immediately, which in turn means that it may be possible to arrest the process. Experimental work with animals has shown that it can be possible to "block" some of these reactions and reduce the final extent of the damage. It is not yet known whether this can be achieved in humans (and obviously the range of experimental research is much more limited), but it may be possible in the future. Cooling patients in ice after head injury, for instance, is being investigated as a way of potentially reducing the damaging chain of intracellular reactions triggered by injury.

In general terms, the larger the area of brain damage, the greater the resulting disability. Nevertheless, it is remarkable how extensive damage can be to the "silent" areas – in particular, the right frontal and right temporal lobes – without producing any noticeable disability.

It is probable that, like any lesion in the brain, the infarct caused by a stroke has a central core of irreversible damage and an outer area of reversible, temporary damage. The brain cells on the edges of the infarct stop working immediately after the stroke, then struggle back to work over the next few months, which is why physiotherapy can play a part in recovery.

The nature of the disability that results from a brain injury is influential in determining the extent of recovery. A paralyzed arm might ultimately be much less disabling than a subtle degree of personality change, despite the fact that such invisible damage is less immediately obvious.

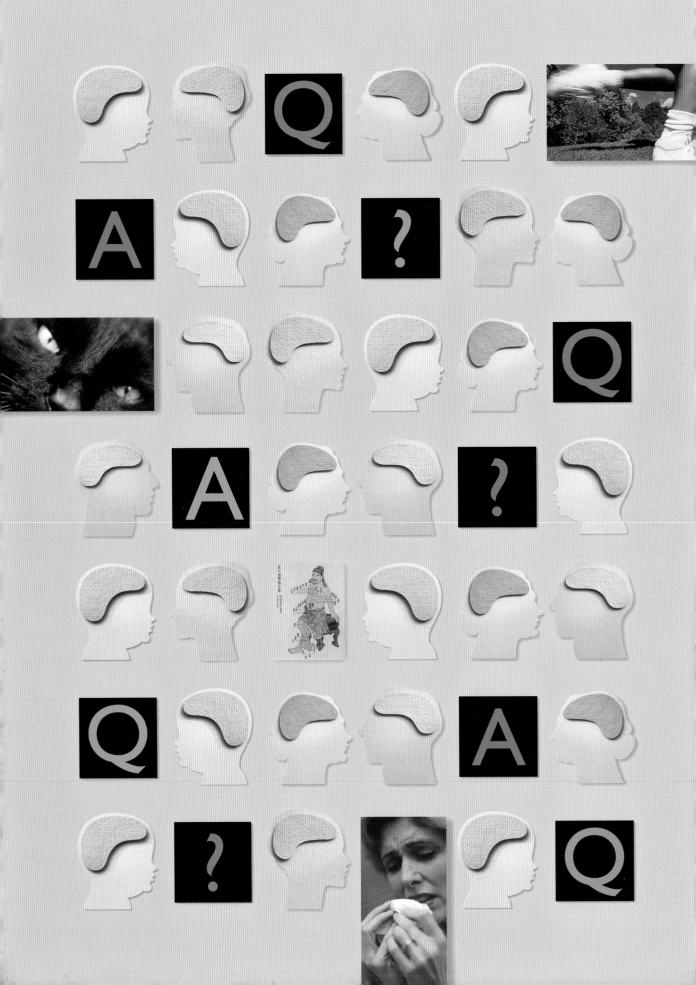

chapter six

questions and answers

Neurological research has benefited from advances in technology, and so we can now answer more questions than ever before about the workings of the brain.

Q

How and where are memories stored?

ABOVE The brain is better understood now than it ever has been, although a lot of areas of the map are still missing.

Q

Is intelligence related to brain size?

Q

Where does the seat of consciousness reside?

A One of the most famous patients in the world is known as H.M. In 1953 he underwent surgery that damaged the temporal lobes on both sides of his brain. From then on, he suffered from devastating amnesia. He could remember events perfectly well that had occurred before the operation, so his long-term memory store was apparently intact. He could also remember telephone numbers long enough to dial them, so his short-term memory store was intact, too. But he seemed unable to form new long-term memories normally. Some part of his memory system had been irreparably damaged. This is a particularly clear demonstration of a basic fact about memory. Different components of memory depend on different regions of the brain, so brain damage can affect some components while sparing others. It is now widely agreed that we have multiple memory-storage systems that operate in parallel with each other. Memory circuits are made up of interconnected modules, and within each module the pattern of connections between the brain cells is used for storing information. So there is no one place where memory is stored.

A Brain size is determined by body size. Einstein's brain would have been much smaller than that of a hefty basketball player, since Einstein was a little guy. Similarly, the female brain is on average smaller than the male brain, simply because women's bodies are generally smaller than men's. But slightly built men and women, in general, are of course no less intelligent than larger people. Intelligence is partly determined by speed of mental processing, which depends mainly on the efficiency and intricacy of the connections between the neurons in a person's brain.

ABOVE The size of your brain is in proportion with the size of your body.

A We know that if parts of the brainstem are damaged or if the cerebral cortex suffers extensive damage, consciousness will be impaired. Also, that the more extensively the cerebral cortex is damaged, the less responsive, less alert, and less attentive we become. However, nobody knows for certain whether consciousness is located in specific areas of the brain, or whether it is a property of the brain as a whole. The view of consciousness as a monitoring function, like a TV producer watching a bank of TV screens in a studio control room, is no longer sustainable. We now know that all the regions of the brain are massively interconnected. At our present level of understanding, we can only surmise that consciousness is a property of the cerebral cortex as a whole.

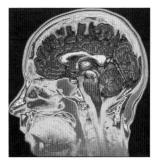

Consciousness is a product of all parts of the brain working together. No single area is essential, and there are many cortical functions – partic-

ABOVE Consciousness is a function of the whole brain working together.

ularly some of the ones concerned with control of movement – that are automatic and do not involve consciousness in any way.

Q

Can non-human animals or computers be self-aware? If so, do we have any means of discovering why this is so?

A Although I am aware that I am writing this sentence, I have difficulty defining the nature of that awareness. Similarly, although I am conscious of what I am doing, that doesn't help to explain the concept of self-awareness, since the nature of consciousness is not yet fully understood. It is therefore difficult to formulate criteria for judging whether non-human animals are capable of being "self-aware," let alone computers. If it were not for the fact that we consider consciousness and awareness to be important characteristics of what it means to be human, we probably wouldn't even think of asking such a question at all.

Q

What happens to the brain's synapses when they are affected by hallucinogenic drugs?

A Drugs such as LSD, psilocybin, and mescaline produce dramatically altered states of perception, accompanied by unusual sensory experiences. Often users experience synesthesia – a state in which sensations such as vision, hearing, smell, and taste become blurred or exchanged. Elucidation of where the hallucinogens act at a cellular level is helping scientists to understand both the mode of action of these drugs and how perception is processed within the brain.

Early research revealed that both LSD and psilocybin (which are structural analogues of the body's endogenous 5-HT) slow down the firing of neurons within the raphe nucleus that release 5-HT. It was suggested that this slowing down occurred as a consequence of the hallucinogens' action on a particular inhibitory subset of 5-HT receptors – which would reduce the inhibitory effect of these neurons on the areas of the cortex believed to be involved in perception. In addition, more recent studies have shown that all hallucinogens increase the rate of firing of the noradrenalin-releasing neurons in the locus coeruleus.

Where does the brain end and the spinal cord begin?

The brain and the spinal cord together form the central nervous system, as opposed to the peripheral nervous system – the name given to the nerves branching out from the brain and spinal cord, to connect them with the other parts of the body. In terms of "architecture" and function, the brain and spinal cord are best understood as a unified structure. In terms of anatomical description (equivalent to defining where the Atlantic Ocean stops and the Antarctic Ocean starts), the spinal cord begins at the foramen magnum (Latin for "large hole") – the gap at the base of the skull. After passing upward through the foramen magnum, it becomes the brainstem.

What is the evolutionary purpose of emotion?

Humans are very sociable animals. Our interactions with one another are an extraordinarily important part of our lives; indeed, much of our success as a species comes from our ability to operate in groups, with a division of labor and with cultural transmission of skills (meaning that skills can be handed down directly from one generation to the next). For a long-lived, slow-breeding species like ours, this leads to much faster evolution of behavioral traits than would be achieved through genetic selection alone.

Emotions help to structure our interactions with other humans, as well as facilitating interactions with other aspects of our environment. For example, love helps to insure that we look after our slow-developing babies. Babies are well designed (or in evolutionary terms, well selected) for interacting with their parents so as to inspire love in them – and parents are designed to respond. So emotions provide ways to cement human groups together. They work for our benefit in other ways, too. They can, for example, provide control at a distance. If you are bitten by a dog, you may come to fear and avoid dogs: fear helps you make sure you don't get bitten again.

LEFT Emotions are an important part of our successful evolution as social creatures.

Why is the brain situated in the head?

It's arguable that the brain does not have to be in the head, any more than an airplane's flight computer has to be in the cockpit. Indeed, in many lower animals the brain is at the back of the body. But in vertebrates the head is the most logical place to put the brain, for several reasons. It makes sense for it to be close to the nose, eyes, and ears – and, especially in four-legged animals, these need to be at the front of the body in order to inspect the world efficiently. In addition, because the brain has the consistency of gelatin, it needs the hard bone "helmet" of the skull to protect it.

Q

Are there any rational explanations for extrasensory perception and telekinesis?

A The scientific view of the world is based on evidence and testability. The idea that we have the power to influence the physical world by thought alone is an attractive one, but there is a striking lack of testable evidence that such phenomena exist.

Extrasensory perception implies the capacity to acquire information by means other than sight, hearing, smell, taste, or touch – for example, being able to identify a picture that someone is looking at in another city or to "sense" what is happening in another room. Telekinesis is the ability to make objects move without touching them. Most examples that have been claimed are either fraudulent or can be explained as coincidences. However, it is difficult to prove that something cannot happen, and there are senses in other animals (such as a magnetic sense) that humans do not possess. It is therefore possible, though unlikely, that other human senses may one day be discovered.

Q

Why can't I remember very much the morning after a night on the town?

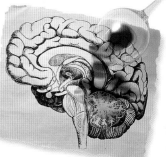

ABOVE Alcohol is a drug, so it interferes with brain functions such as memory retention.

A There are two reasons why you may find it hard to remember what happened after you have had too much to drink. The first is that some drugs interfere with the neural activities that underlie memory formation: under their influence, memories simply don't get stored in the first place. For instance, a lot of anesthetics and some of the drugs used as premedication in surgery seem to block memory formation. High levels of alcohol probably have a similar effect.

The second reason is completely unrelated to the first. Sometimes memories are perfectly well stored, but are inaccessible. This is because our memories are most easily recalled within the "learning context" in which they were originally formed. If you put something down and can't remember where you've put it, the best way to jog your memory is to try to retrace your steps. The "external context" of the world around us has long been recognized as a powerful determinant in memory retrieval, and it is now clear that the state of your own brain – what might be termed the "internal context" – can be just as powerful. This is true of our moods: depressed patients often can't recall experiences they had when they weren't depressed, but remember other depressing experiences only too clearly. Similarly, things experienced under the influence of some drugs can sometimes only be recalled when we are once again under their influence. So, sometimes, the hair of the dog may help…

Q

Why are we not conscious of the workings of our own viscera?

A While we are conscious of the actions of our skeletal muscles, we have no awareness of the actions of our visceral tissues and organs. The liver, heart, blood vessels, glands, and other parts of the visceral or autonomic motor system operate automatically, without voluntary conscious control. This means that our vital organs are able to maintain a steady state even when we are unconscious, and also allows the conscious mind to concentrate on other matters, such as control of the skeletal motor system.

Another reason why the viscera are not under conscious control appears to be the "geography" of the areas that control the autonomic motor system. The overall control – the nucleus of the solitary tract – is located in the brainstem, where it can closely monitor the activity of other brainstem nuclei, which control functions such as heart rate, temperature, and respiration. In addition, it commands the hypothalamus, another region of the brain that is involved in autonomic control – particularly via its ability to influence hormonal release. Last, the nucleus of the solitary tract receives sensory inputs from the viscera, which allows it to act as the command centre of the autonomic motor system. The location of the solitary tract at a distance from the cerebral cortex means that its nucleus is able to regulate the autonomic motor system in the absence of conscious control.

ABOVE Operations to relieve pressure on the brain have been known for centuries.

Q

Is there a scientific basis for the practice of trepanning?

A Ancient skulls found by archeologists reveal that many thousands of years ago some people had their skulls opened by crude surgical techniques while still alive. The healing of the edges of the opening in the bone indicate that the patients must have survived. It is not known why these surgical operations were performed, and we can only speculate as to whether they were done for "psychological" reasons (exorcizing evil spirits and the like) or for "medical" reasons.

The discovery of these skulls is very intriguing because trepanning is a long-established part of standard Western medical practice. It is fairly common for a blood clot to form on the surface of the brain, usually due to a head injury. The resulting pressure on the brain can cause confusion, paralysis, coma, and death. If the blood clot is liquid, it can be drained out by simply drilling a hole in the skull, and the patient will often make a good recovery. It is tempting to speculate that early doctors discovered this thousands of years ago.

Q

Is anything known about the 80 percent of the brain that is supposedly unused?

A We use the entirety of our brains almost all of the time. The myth that 80 percent is unused derived from a popular misinterpretation of some experiments carried out by Karl Lashley and others in the 1920s. They found that after removing a large part of a rat's brain (though not as much as 80 percent), it could still run through a maze it had learned to navigate before the operation. However, the time it took to get through the maze, and also the time it took to learn a new one, became progressively longer as each bit of the brain was removed. These experiments in fact demonstrated that even a rat needs its entire brain for optimum performance. For our own part, we certainly need the whole of ours, though it was once widely believed that the right ("minor") hemisphere of the cerebral cortex was redundant.

Nevertheless, it is possible to function with only one hemisphere if the other has to be excised (for example, to remove an epileptic focus), provided that the loss occurs early in life. If an adult loses even a small part of the cerebral cortex, their abilities are irretrievably impaired. With adults, left-hemisphere lesions result in the deterioration of verbal and logical abilities; after right-hemisphere damage, visuospatial skills diminish, and there may be personality changes due to flattening of the emotions.

Q

What are dreams for?

A From antiquity to modern times, there has been a great deal of speculation about the purpose and significance of dreams. Indeed, a whole school of psychotherapy, psychoanalysis, developed around the notion that dreams represent the purging of disturbing thoughts that are not retrievable during the conscious waking state. While science now understands more about the "how" of dream sleep, the question of why it occurs remains very much unanswered. The major advances in this area have largely been due to the discovery of a particular phase of sleep during which almost all dreaming occurs. Known as REM sleep, because of the rapid eye movements that take place throughout its duration, it occurs many times during any normal period of sleep and with increasing frequency as sleep progresses.

ABOVE The purpose and meaning of dreams have been the subject of intense speculation.

Because of its close correlation with dreaming, REM sleep has become the focus of investigation into the purpose of dreams. Sleep experiments have shown that it is possible to interrupt REM sleep for many days without decreasing the subject's mental or physiological performance in any way. Similarly, patients undergoing chronic drug treatments that incidentally abolish REM sleep show no psychological consequences. On the other hand, there is evidence indicating that REM sleep is physiologically necessary, as a significant increase in REM sleep occurs after any period of deprivation. It has yet to be discovered, however, what the nature of this requirement for dreaming is.

Is the brain computational or non-computational?

This is a highly controversial question. At one level the answer is obviously "yes," because the brain processes data according to a neural information-processing program. However, there is considerable disagreement as to how to describe this information-processing capacity. Some researchers regard the brain as operating like a conventional computer program, manipulating symbols according to a set of well-defined rules. Others think this approach is fundamentally wrong, and instead view the basic operations of the brain in a non-symbolic manner. So the jury is still out.

If the brain of a cat was transplanted into the body of a sheep, would the hybrid chase string and eat fish?

Behavior is produced by the brain – so if you transplant a brain, you transplant behavior as well. So the hybrid would be a cat in sheep's clothing, although the sheep-cat would be ill-equipped in many ways for its new lifestyle. It's doubtful, for instance, that it would be very good at catching mice.

RIGHT The brain of an animal is fundamental to how it behaves.

If brain waves are made of electricity, where is the battery?

As with all the other organs in the body, the brain's "battery" is the "sodium pump," which pumps sodium ions out of our nerve cells and potassium ions back in. This is powered by energy derived from the oxidation of glucose. The pump's separation of sodium and potassium means that if sodium channels in the nerve membrane open, positively charged sodium ions rush in. This sodium current is the main electric current by which messages are sent from one part of the brain to another.

The recording of "brain waves" by electroencephalography (EEG) measures the summation of synaptic potentials from cortical pyramidal neurons that are lying beneath the electrodes attached to the scalp. The "battery" that drives these waves is the sodium/potassium transporter located within the neuronal membrane. This enzyme uses energy to transport sodium and potassium ions across the membrane, resulting in the formation of an electrochemical gradient. Whenever an ion channel opens, often in response to a neurotransmitter, the ions have a bridge through which they can pass from one side of the membrane to the other, driven by the established electrochemical gradient. It is a summation of these ionic currents that is recorded by EEG.

LEFT The brain runs on electricity that comes from the transfer of positively charged sodium ions through nerve cells.

ABOVE Language is one function that shows left-hemisphere localization in most people.

Q

Is the left brain/right brain polarity the same for left-handed people?

A The brain appears to have a lateral specialization of function for many tasks. Perhaps the best understood is the dominance of the left hemisphere in language. In right-handed people, speech is almost always localized to the left side of the brain. In contrast, experiments using a barbiturate to temporarily suppress one side of the brain have confirmed that left-handed people show a difference in distribution of language. In 70 percent of those tested, speech was localized to the left hemisphere, but in the remaining cases it was found to be either localized to the right side of the brain or distributed across both hemispheres. The relationship between handedness and left/right brain polarity is not yet fully understood.

Q

How do the chemicals in pharmaceutical drugs cross the blood-brain interface?

A The administration of neuroactive drugs presents a major dilemma, because the blood-brain barrier proves a formidable obstacle to any molecule that is to pass from the bloodstream into the brain. Many drugs that would otherwise be powerful agents are rendered ineffective by their inability to target the central nervous system. There are, however, two methods of entry across this barrier that allow for the distribution of neuroactive compounds to the brain.

The blood-brain barrier has a number of functions, among them the protection of the brain from any noxious substances outside it and the removal of potentially toxic waste products, as well as maintaining a buffered, secure environment in which the neurons can survive. To this end, the cells that line the blood capillaries in the brain have very tight junctions, which even prevent the flow of small ions from the blood to the brain and vice versa. In order to cross the blood-brain barrier, a molecule must either have a specific transporter in these "guard" cells or else be lipid-soluble enough to diffuse across their membranes.

An example of the former is L-DOPA, a drug that has become the mainstay of treatment for Parkinson's disease. L-DOPA is carried across the barrier by an amino-acid transporter and then converted to dopamine – whereas dopamine itself is not recognized by any such transporter and so cannot access the brain.

Heroin is a classic example of the second way of crossing the blood-brain barrier. Because it is a small hydrophobic molecule, it is able to pass through the membranes of the cells that protect the brain – whereas morphine, from which heroin is derived, is more water-soluble and so cannot cross the barrier. Once across, the components of the heroin molecule that make it fat-soluble are cleaved, giving the active morphine molecule.

ABOVE Drugs that are directed at the brain need to negotiate the blood-brain barrier.

Q Why does brain surgery tickle but not hurt, when headaches can be almost unbearable?

A The brain itself has no sensations. If you touch the surface of somebody's brain when they are awake, they will not feel anything. However, if some of the veins that run from the brain to the meninges (the membrane that covers the brain) are pulled on, quite severe pain is felt. The reason is that the structures around the brain – skin, blood vessels, meninges – register pain, but the brain itself does not. Headaches derive from these structures, rather than from the brain itself. However, the exact mechanism of migraine (a severe headache preceded by a brief disturbance of brain function, usually signaled by flashing lights) is not yet understood.

Q What are the factors that keep the brain healthy?

A The crucial thing is to keep using it. The brain is very adaptable, and we are constantly finding further examples of its potential for reorganization and change. On the plus side, we already know that nerve cells in the brain can make new connections in response to damage; and that existing connections continually change as a result of experience. We have great potential for constructive reorganization. To give just one example, when adults learn new tasks requiring an unusual dexterity and sensitivity in the fingers, the area of the brain activated by finger stimulation and movement measurably increases.

On the minus side, as we age we lose brain cells; and even the ones that we retain lose some of their complexity. Just as oak trees lose first twigs and then branches as they age, leaving a much less intricate tree, so the structures through which brain cells get their inputs become less complex, which reduces their potential. Similarly, head injuries and severe chronic stress tend to "prune" some of the brain cells.

How can you boost the plus side and keep the minus side in check? Practicing existing skills and acquiring new ones seem to help maintain brain-cell complexity. So the more active the brain, the better it lasts.

Q

Why does the brain appear to become dull after several hours of sustained work, and feel refreshed after a relatively short break?

ABOVE Activity improves blood flow to the muscles, but we don't know whether thinking improves the blood supply to the brain.

A Most of the time, the brain consumes more energy than any other organ – but, unlike muscle, it can't store much energy. When any part of the brain is active, it requires more blood flow (which is why imaging is able to indicate which parts of the brain perform different functions). However, because the brain is enclosed in a rigid skull, the overall blood flow to the brain is not able to increase very much. So after periods of intense mental effort, the energy stores are low and have to be replenished by a short period of rest.

The brain consumes energy, and brain scans show that when we are thinking, blood flow increases to the parts of the brain being used. We know that one of the physical consequences of athletic training is an improved blood supply to muscles, so they tire less quickly, but it is not yet known whether similar considerations apply to the brain.

Q

Leonardo da Vinci was able to write "backward." Why do some people have this ability?

A Probably, Leonardo da Vinci could write backward because he was ambidextrous. Most of us are more "dexterous" with the right hand (only ten percent of us are left-handed) and, since we are taught to write from left to right, become polarized for that direction. But ambidextrous people are not so polarized, and so can often mirror-write. Interestingly, in Israel, many bilinguals who as children were taught to write Hebrew from right to left and English from left to right are able to write both languages in both directions. But mirror-writing isn't always an advantage. The lack of polarity means that it is difficult to learn which is the "correct" way to write; and children with reading difficulties (developmental dyslexics) frequently mirror-write. Likewise, some stroke patients start mirror-writing without realizing it.

Is it possible to give an estimate of how much of the brain's functioning is currently understood by neurological science?

A The gap between what we understand about the brain and what remains to be explained is probably comparable to the gap between understanding something about bricks and understanding the entire history of architecture. That is to say, we have only begun to scratch the surface in our exploration of the brain's complexities. Great advances have been made recently as a result of improved brain imaging and scanning equipment.

We understand basic sensory and motor processes in great detail, but know much less about the transfer of information between the two. Since 90 percent of the human brain is devoted to sensorimotor transformations, a rough estimate would be that we understand only ten percent of its functions.

Human DNA is said to differ from that of chimpanzees by less than one percent. Is there a similar difference between the brains of chimps and humans?

A DNA can be thought of as a set of building instructions. It's a complete set, too: it tells you how to build a whole animal. The basic building blocks from which all mammals are constructed are very similar, and they are all specified in DNA. So, much of the instruction set has to be almost exactly the same. However, the DNA also specifies how to combine those blocks to build a brain; and just as you can construct very different buildings from identical components, you can construct very different brains from the same basic materials.

Add to this the fact that brains do a lot of self-organizing during development, and it becomes clear that the differences are likely to get magnified as development contin-ues. After all, you start with a solitary cell and end up with billions of interacting cells. So a very small difference in the basic building

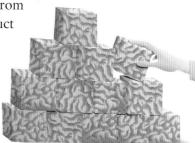

ABOVE The DNA building blocks used in human and animal brains are deceptively similar; it's the connections and instructions that make the big difference.

instructions can lead to a very big difference in the final product: a one percent difference at the beginning can lead to an enor-mous difference at the end. So although chimpanzees are the closest relatives to human beings, humans are not just chim-panzees with 101 percent brain power.

Most of the body's functions begin a long decline after the age of 18, but the brain appears to become more capable as time goes on. Why should that be so?

What is the explanation for the strong visual and auditory delusions that affect people with certain medical conditions, including Alzheimer's disease, depression, and schizophrenia?

What is a migraine?

 The final layer of myelin sheathing (the insulation that allows signals to pass quickly along the axons of nerve cells) on the fibers that link the two cerebral hemispheres together, and those that supply the cerebellum (one of the motor centers), is not completed until our mid-twenties – which may be why mathematicians and sportspeople generally don't reach their peak until then. But even after this time the brain, unlike other organs, continues to mature through experience. Each memory involves the slight reshaping of thousands of connections between nerve cells, and of course this goes on throughout life. Thus any activity that depends on mental experience – such as philosophy, medicine, or art – matures and hopefully improves with age, until eventually these processes begin to deteriorate.

ABOVE Unlike other forms of progressive organic decay, the brain's function can improve with age.

Because visual and auditory hallucinations so often occur in Alzheimer's disease, depression, and schizophrenia, the presence of such delusions play a prominent role in the diagnosis of these diseases. Although the cause of these hallucinations remains uncertain, modern imaging techniques have helped to shed some light on why they occur.

One possible explanation is an abnormal level of dopamine activity in the mesolimbic pathway – part of the limbic system, which has long been thought of as playing a role in emotions and memory. Overactivation of a particular subgroup of dopamine receptors in the temporal cortex by this pathway is thought to be the underlying cause of the hallucinations. Antipsychotic drugs that treat the positive symptoms of schizophrenia are known to block these receptors; and imaging studies have shown an abnormal sensitivity to speech in the temporal cortex of schizophrenic patients. Moreover, in Alzheimer's disease there is an almost complete loss of these types of receptors in the temporal cortex.

There are many different kinds of headache recognized by doctors. Migraine is a severe headache usually accompanied by nausea and sometimes by vomiting; it is episodic and can last up to 24 hours. A large number of people suffer from frequent or occasional attacks.

With "classical" migraine, the headache is preceded by transient neurological symptoms, which last 10 to 15 minutes. The most common symptom is loss of central vision, accompanied

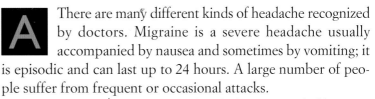

by flashing zigzag lights. This visual disturbance subsides and is then replaced by a severe headache. So-called "common" migraine is a similar kind of headache, but without these neurological symptoms. The mechanisms of migraine are not yet understood, but attacks can sometimes be stopped by treatment with drugs that reduce the effect of the neurotransmitter serotonin, if taken soon after the symptoms start.

Q

What happens during an epileptic seizure?

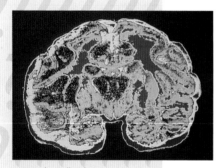

ABOVE An epileptic attack is something like an electrical storm happening in the brain.

A An epileptic seizure is a form of electric storm that starts in one part of the cerebral hemispheres (as opposed to the brainstem or cerebellum) and can spread to other parts of the brain. We still do not understand the mechanisms involved, despite a great deal of research and the fact that between one percent and two percent of the population experience an epileptic attack at some point in their life.

Epilepsy develops if one area of the brain becomes "electrically unstable." This is usually caused by physical damage such as birth trauma (the effects of which can become apparent many years after birth), head injury, infection, or a brain tumor. It can also be caused by metabolic problems, such as lack of oxygen getting to the brain; and in a few susceptible individuals, by flashing lights.

If an area of the brain suffers an epileptic seizure, overactivity of that part of the brain results. For instance, if the seizure starts in the left motor area, the right side of the body will start to jerk convulsively. If it starts in the temporal lobes, repetitive ideas or hallucinationlike visions may be experienced. If the electrical disturbance does not travel beyond the area of the brain where it started, the patient will remain conscious and the attack stops within a few minutes. However, if the electrical storm spreads to other parts of the brain, the patient will lose consciousness and collapse; this is what used to be known as a "grand mal siezure," but nowadays is called a generalized seizure.

The usual treatment for epilepsy consists of anticonvulsant drugs that reduce the electrical excitability of the brain. It is not always easy to diagnose, as there are many different forms a seizure may take – some of them surprising. Epileptic attacks arising in the limbic system can cause some people to experience intense religious feelings, with a sense of mystical communion with God, and their life may be profoundly changed as a result. Others have reported experiencing an overwhelming sense of an evil presence. Epilepsy has been suggested as an influence on the creativity of certain writers such as Fyodor Dostoevsky, Gustave Flaubert, and Lord Byron.

Is there any such thing as a fair intelligence test?

What is the purpose of laughter? And why is a sense of humor found only in humans?

All intelligence tests are based on ability to perform tasks. Since task performance is experience-dependent, intelligence tests are always influenced by the experiences afforded by the background culture. It would therefore be impossible to create a universal intelligence test that could accurately compare the abilities of people from different cultures.

Humans have a highly developed ability to express and interpret emotions. Emotional expression seems to be innate, its evolutionary selection no doubt reflecting the importance of its role in social communication. Laughter provides a particularly potent communication channel, which not only helps to create group cohesion but also serves as a powerful mechanism for neutralizing or diverting threatening and aggressive behavior. In addition to being extraordinarily sociable creatures, we are the only ones to have developed language to such an extent that we are able to communicate abstract ideas. It is therefore scarcely surprising that we have turned this ability to good use in making jokes.

I have sometimes wondered whether the human sense of the absurd – which depends upon a conception of how something differs from the way we think it ought to be – constitutes a further fundamental difference between human beings and other animals. Various animals can learn to self-administer certain drugs, such as nicotine, alcohol, and cocaine, that directly affect the reward systems of the brain. However, they apparently cannot be encouraged to self-administer hallucinogenic drugs, such as LSD or mescaline. Could it be that humans take these drugs because they find distortions of the way the world ought to be in some way entertaining – whereas animals, which do not share human beings' conceptual abilities, simply find such distortions frightening?

ABOVE Laughing at life is a uniquely human response, a part of our evolution as social animals.

We laugh when there is incongruity between what we expect and what actually happens, unless the outcome is frightening. Although nowadays a sense of humor is seen as a desirable characteristic, that has not always been so; for example, there is very little humor in the Bible, and even in the eighteenth century too much laughter was considered coarse and ungentlemanly. Today most of us like to think that we have an above-average sense of humor and that this is healthy; and laughter is seen as a defense against depression.

Hormones such as adrenalin build up in anticipation of threatening situations, and it may be that the original physiological function of laughter was to help dissipate those hormones when the threat disappears. Something very like laughter can be seen in the noisy displacement activities of monkeys after they have been in confrontational situations.

What are the different types of brain scan, and what do they tell us?

A There are three principal kinds of modern brain scan: CAT or CT (computerized axial tomography), MRI (magnetic resonance imaging), and PET (positron emission tomography). They each are based upon different physical processes and have slightly different uses. Each method of scanning produces two-dimensional pictures of the brain, as a series of "slices," rather like the slices of a sliced tomato. CAT scanning shows the physical structure of the brain and can reveal details measuring a millimeter or two across. MRI scanning does the same, but is also able to show blood flow. This means that it can be used "functionally." For instance, when you move an arm or leg, special "sequences" of MRI indicate the increased blood flow to the parts of the brain responsible for movement. MRI cannot show "thoughts" as such, but it is able to reveal the increase in blood flow to the "speech areas" of the brain prompted by reading or writing. PET scanning is used in roughly the same way. Both CAT and MRI scanning are used by doctors to help in investigating neurological illnesses.

ABOVE Brain scans give us information about functioning brains that is often more useful than postmortem study.

The ability to see into the living brain is a recent one, and the technology that lets us do it is developing very fast. Previously our information about the brain came from postmortem dissections. Early attempts to use X-rays to show the structures of the brain depended on injecting a special dye into the carotid arteries that supply the brain. This technique allows the brain's blood vessels to be seen, and can be used to reveal cancerous tumors because they develop their own rich blood supplies.

The first technique that reliably showed up brain tissues themselves was the CAT scan. Although this still uses X-rays, it employs complex computer programs to construct images that are much clearer than the ones produced by simpler X-ray equipment. With CAT scanning, for instance, neurologists are able to measure the shrinkage of the brain that accompanies Alzheimer's disease.

More recently, two much more sophisticated methods have emerged. MRI, which is now used quite widely for clinic purposes, relies on signals produced by surrounding the head (or any other part of the body) with intense magnetic fields. It has given the clearest pictures yet of the structures of the brain. MRI can be used to examine the area damaged by a suspected stroke, or the more subtle damage produced by multiple sclerosis; and, as well as showing structure, it can measure function.

Functional MRI (fMRI) is possible because when a particular part of the brain increases its activity, the blood flow to that area increases as well. Changes in blood flow and blood oxygen levels change the fMRI signal. So it is now possible to see what happens in the brain when we think. At present fMRI is still mainly a research tool, rather than a clinical one.

PET scanning provides an alternative functional imaging system. It can detect blood flow changes (although with less precision than fMRI) and can also be used to show which areas of the brain take up particular drugs or chemicals. At the moment it is largely a research tool, but like fMRI it has clinical potential.

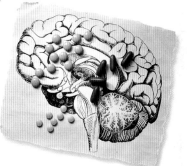

ABOVE Barbiturate sleeping pills have largely given way to the safer benzodiasepines.

Q

How do sleeping pills work?

A Drugs prescribed as sleeping pills fall into two distinct groups, the barbiturates and the benzodiazepines. Both groups act to modulate the GABA "A" receptor *(see pages 96–7)*, although they work by different mechanisms. As a result, activity of this receptor channel increases, although it is not yet known on which cells increased receptor activity must occur in order for the drugs to exert their hypnotic effects.

Barbiturates are historically the older of the two groups of drugs. They are highly sedative, and there is a danger of coma or death occurring at higher doses. For this reason they have been supplanted by the benzodiazepines, which have a much safer pharmacological profile.

In addition to decreasing the time it takes for us to fall asleep, both types of drug reduce the amount of time we spend in REM or "dreaming" sleep. Paradoxically, these drugs seem to improve the more "subjective" effects of sleep to a greater extent than the measurable aspects, such as the amount of time spent in deep sleep. It may be that the benzodiazepines decrease the number of "micro-wakes," thus providing more continuous rather than longer sleep.

Q

**How do lie
detectors work?**

A Lie detectors don't actually show we are lying: they merely indicate how we feel about what we say by measuring the electrical conductivity of the skin. Skin conductivity changes radically when we sweat, because sweat contains salts that are good conductors. Consequently, if something makes us sweat or changes the blood flow through our skin, the lie detector can detect it. Our emotions have powerful effects on our skin: we turn white with rage, we blush with embarrassment, and we break into a cold sweat with fear. This is partly because intense emotions are often associated with a need for action. For instance, if we are frightened, we may need to run or fight, and prepare by directing blood flow away from our skin to our muscles. So emotional changes modify skin conductance, and this is what lie detectors pick up.

The more we believe in the power of lie detectors, the more anxious we will be when we lie and the clearer our emotional responses to lying will become. This suggests how to fool the machine. When you are asked questions to which the answers can be easily verified, answer truthfully, but at the same time think of something extremely embarrassing, or very exciting, in order to produce a blip on the detector. If answers that are obviously truthful produce the same results as ones that may be lies, the test will reveal nothing.

Q

**How do
anesthetics work?**

A Modern surgical procedures are extremely refined in comparison with what was possible even in the relatively recent past. Amazingly precise and complicated operations can now be performed where once the most a surgeon could accomplish was a crude amputation. One of the main reasons for this revolution has been the development of anesthesia. Anesthetic drugs fall into two main categories: general anesthetics, which work at the central level, and local anesthetics, which act peripherally.

General anesthetics act within the brain to eliminate the patient's awareness of sensations of pain. Unlike almost all other classes of drugs, they share no obvious common structure or receptor site. Instead, they appear to act by inserting themselves within cell membranes in such a way that they disrupt the cells' normal functioning. They do this by interacting either with the lipids or the proteins that compose the membrane, though at present we do not know which. In doing so, they reduce transmitter release and the postsynaptic response to the transmitter. It appears that the area where this action is crucial is the reticular formation, a region that is thought to be responsible for general arousal and awareness.

Q

Why are small children better at learning a new language than adults?

Q

Is there anything one can do to prevent or delay the onset of Alzheimer's disease?

Local anesthetics, on the other hand, act by blocking the conduction of pain signals from peripheral pain receptors to the central nervous system. They mainly do this by inhibiting the voltage-gated sodium channels that propagate signals along the conduction fibers. This appears to be due to one of two mechanisms. First, they may be able to insert themselves into the membrane, much as general anesthetics do, which produces a dysfunction in membrane operation. Of greater importance, however, is their ability to directly "plug" the pores of these channels, thus hindering the passage of any sodium ions and preventing conduction.

A By the age of 12 months, infants have discovered which sound contrasts (phonemes) are used to convey meaning in their native language. After this time, they lose the ability to distinguish non-native speech contrasts. Similarly, adult speakers are not able to articulate these differences reliably – which results in the characteristic mispronunciations of a language by foreign speakers. In addition, the tonal accents of a language are acquired in early childhood and are difficult to remove once learned.

A Some cases of Alzheimer's disease are genetic, but the great majority aren't. There are a number of factors associated with later onset of Alzheimer's or a slower course of the disease. Women tend to get Alzheimer's later than men do, and it now looks as though female hormone replacement therapy can increase this tendency. People who take anti-inflammatory drugs regularly, for conditions such as rheumatoid arthritis, seem to have a lower risk of developing Alzheimer's. However, the anti-inflammatory drugs used at

ABOVE Alzheimer's is a scourge of old age, but it is not inevitable.

present can cause bleeding in the stomach and should not be taken regularly except on medical recommendation.

Diet may also be of help. Antioxidant vitamins like Vitamin C and Vitamin E may reduce nerve-cell damage. Recent research suggests that folic acid may help to fend off the disease, too. This occurs in cabbage and liver. Finally, if you're reluctant to eat liver and can't stand greens, you may benefit from a glass of red wine each day. It is now thought that moderate wine-drinking not only protects against heart disease, but also reduces the chances of suffering from neurodegenerative diseases such as Alzheimer's.

Q Is there a
connection
between our
immune system and
our state of mental
health? Why do
feelings of
depression seem to
affect our general
health?

ABOVE There is some evidence
that a positive psychological
outlook has an effect on our
physical health.

A The various parts of the
"immune system" – such as
the spleen, thymus, and
bone marrow – have nerve connections to the central nervous system.
Given that "thought is physical,"
there is, in principle, no reason why
our mental state should not influence
our immunity and susceptibility to
disease. However, it is probably only
one influence among others that
determine whether or not we become
ill. There is no evidence that state of mind is more important
than anything else in determining whether you catch a cold or
develop cancer.

A fundamental aspect of what is known as complementary
medicine is the belief that thoughts and feelings can control
physical health (although clearly it is difficult to establish the
dividing line between "physical" and "mental" health). There is
little evidence that such mechanisms play a significant role in the
majority of people, though there is suggestive evidence that they
contribute to some extent. One of the consequences of modern
medical technology is that serious illnesses are now often diagnosed at a much earlier stage than was possible in the past, while
the presenting symptoms are still relatively trivial. This has produced a considerable population of people who have been told
they have a potentially fatal illness such as cancer, even though
they feel perfectly well in themselves. This inevitably leads to
intense stress and anxiety, and a very understandable wish to find
alternatives to the conventional medical treatment, which they
may have already received and which they know may well prove
ultimately ineffective.

Substantial components of the immune system are under the
direct control of the brain. When we are stressed, the brain gives
a signal to release stress hormones – which have many effects,
among them suppression of immune responses. Stress hormones
also directly affect brain function, through feedback loops: after
all, the brain needs to know whether anything has happened in
response to its signals. So it's not at all surprising that our
mental state and the immune system are linked. For example,
there's evidence that athletes are particularly susceptible to viral
infections, such as colds and flu, and it is quite possible that the
stresses of intense training and competition outweigh the advantages of being physically very fit. There's also evidence that stress
can exacerbate skin conditions, such as psoriasis, and accelerate
the progress of various chronic conditions.

ABOVE Stress can cause a
suppression of our immune
responses which can lead to
infections such as flu.

But intense, prolonged stress doesn't just reduce the protection afforded by our immune system. It is known to cause brain damage in animals – and evidence suggests that it has the same effect in humans, too. This is probably because prolonged high levels of stress hormones are toxic to brain cells. Adult susceptibilities to these effects depend partly on developmental factors: animals that have experienced short periods of mild stress during development seem to do better than those whose development has been free from stress. So it would appear that the stress-hormone system has to be "tuned" while you are growing up in order to maximize its benefit for the rest of your life.

ABOVE Stress hormones are toxic to brain cells after too long an exposure.

There are certainly many connections between the nervous and immune systems. Both are derived from the same layer of cells in the embryo; both detect and react to external stimuli; and both systems employ many of the same chemical transmitters and hormones. All the immune organs are equipped with nerves that can turn their productivity up or down. This means that there are a great many ways in which immune responses can be modulated by the nervous system – production of antibodies, for example, increases during the night and wanes during the day. Our mood can therefore very easily affect immune responses and physical health. In particular, depression increases vulnerability to viral infection, and conversely such infections often trigger depression.

Q

What happens when I faint?

A Fainting occurs when there is a brief reduction in the flow of blood to the brain. It can occur with extreme emotion, probably due to slowing of the heart rate – caused by the emotion stimulating the vagus nerve, which controls heart beat. It can also happen when you stand up suddenly from a sitting position, if the reflexes responsible for pumping blood up to the brain are caught napping. You are more likely to faint when you are hot, because more blood is diverted to the skin in order to keep the body cool, so less blood is available for supplying the brain. When you fall over as a result of fainting, gravity restores your blood flow – so, from that point of view, it is a perfectly safe event. If you feel you are about to faint, sit down and put your head between your knees. Doing so will restore the cerebral blood flow.

Q

What is the "endorphin high" that some sportspeople claim to experience?

A The "endorphin high" has been created and perpetuated by the media – it's a magazine myth. It's true that some of the chemicals made in the central nervous system and in the endocrine glands have opiatelike effects (e.g. endorphin, enkephalin, dynorphin). It's also true that sports and other intense physical activities can make the participant euphoric. But there's no evidence to support the idea that joggers are giving themselves a "high" – let alone becoming addicted to jogging – by stimulating the release of opiatelike chemicals. Perhaps the most important point to bear in mind is that even if sporting activities increase the level of such chemicals in the bloodstream,

ABOVE The "endorphin high" is something of a myth, but jogging still makes you feel good.

it's unlikely that the brain could be influenced: these molecules are simply too big to pass through the cells that line the capillaries of the brain. Furthermore, we don't yet know whether exercise promotes the release of these chemicals inside the brain, as well as in the bloodstream. The few endorphin cells in the brain (as opposed to the pituitary gland) are restricted to a very small part of the hypothalamus – and you can't stick biopsy needles into that part of an athlete.

Q

What are the long-term effects of taking ecstasy?

A Ecstasy (MDMA) was once touted as a safe modern recreational drug. It has become increasingly apparent, however, that it is far from safe – even relatively small amounts can have long-lasting deleterious effects on the central nervous system. Experiments in animals have shown that MDMA destroys the axon terminals of neurons that contain 5-HT. The regions where this destruction is greatest include the hippocampus, the cortex, and the corpus striatum.

Because of the role of 5-HT in learning and memory, and the importance of the hippocampus in these processes, the search for harmful effects in human ecstasy users has focused on memory functions. It has been established beyond doubt that exposure to ecstasy results in selective memory impairments, even in very infrequent users; but there still remains much work to be done in order to determine whether ecstasy use leads to other cognitive defects.

The reason for the 5-HT neurotoxicity of MDMA is not fully understood, but it is thought to involve interaction of the drug with neurons containing dopamine as well as with ones containing 5-HT. It has recently been suggested that MDMA causes an increased release of both of these neurotransmitters (which would account for the heightened sense of wellbeing reported by users). It is thought that the increased 5-HT release amplifies the amount of dopamine released, which is in turn aberrantly taken up into the depleted 5-HT terminals. The enzyme that normally breaks down 5-HT then does the same to the dopamine, but with the added production of free radicals that lead to degeneration of the 5-HT terminals. This theory has the virtue of incorporating all the information concerning MDMA gleaned so far, though whether experimental research will confirm it remains to be seen.

Q

How can I improve my memory?

A The most effective way of keeping our mental faculties, in general, in good condition is to make use of them. This applies equally to memory. Waiters in restaurants, for instance, who regularly have to remember lists of food orders, can sometimes develop exceptionally good short-term memories. However, there are many different memory systems in the brain *(see page 132)*, and improving one doesn't automatically improve the others.

There hasn't been much progress in finding drugs or food additives that improve memory. In fact this may even be difficult in principle for a normal brain, though in a number of animal studies glucose has apparently aided learning without producing undesirable side effects. Evolution has probably tuned our memory systems precisely to address our specific circumstances. So obvious possibilities – such as increasing the excitability of the brain's memory areas in order to enhance their

ABOVE Being very good at recalling telephone numbers does not necessarily mean that other aspects of your memory are well developed.

storage functions – might produce overexcitability, which would in turn increase the chances of epileptic seizures.

For a damaged brain, reversing the damage by increasing the level of some missing neurotransmitter might well prove therapeutic. Just such approaches are currently being used to address the problems of Alzheimer's disease. For the rest of us, learning how to use our memory systems effectively is probably the best answer, as well as the simplest.

To remember things effectively, go over them several times at intervals (spaced memorizing tends to last longer than intense periods of cramming). Minimize distraction, and try to relate new information to things you already know well. Some people find that links such as visual imagery are an effective aid.

Why do spinal injuries so often cause paralysis?

 When the bones of the spine are fractured, the spinal cord – which runs through them, in the spinal canal – often gets damaged, too. It is possible, however, to fracture the spine without damaging the spinal cord (whereas it is very unusual to damage the spinal cord in an accident without breaking any of the vertebrae).

The spinal cord carries messages between the brain and the body. So if the cord is damaged, messages sent by the brain to move parts of the body, such as the arms and legs, will fail to reach them. The result is paralysis. Severe paralysis caused by complete disruption of the nerves cannot be remedied; but partial paralysis resulting from injury, without complete disruption, can get better.

Is the use of lobotomy ever justifiable?

Strictly, the term lobotomy means the surgical removal of an entire lobe of the brain. But the word is often used to mean any kind of operation on the brain performed to remedy "mental" as opposed to "physical" illness. Psychosurgery is another name given to treatment of this kind, which involves destruction of brain tissue.

The extensive destruction of brain tissue involved in a lobotomy can never be justified. Indeed, it is now recognized that the results of such radical surgery carried out during the first half of the twentieth century were no better than the illnesses they were supposed to treat. Very limited removal of areas of brain tissue, on the other hand, can be beneficial in conditions such as epilepsy and Parkinson's disease. Some clinicians argue that it can also help in some cases of severe depression. Nevertheless, although depressive illnesses can be fatal, through suicide, psychosurgery produces irreversible changes in the brain, so should only be contemplated when all other means of treatment have failed and the patient's life is at risk.

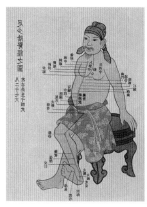

ABOVE Acupuncture is now quite widely used, but still not wholly understood.

How does acupuncture work?

Although acupuncture has been used in China since ancient times for pain relief and treatment of diseases, its acceptance in the West has been slow, partly because of a lack of understanding of how it works. However, it has begun to be used for pain relief and also in the treatment of drug addiction. Its use in treating mental illness remains limited, although studies have outlined its efficacy in treating some conditions such as depression and schizophrenia.

Recent research indicates that acupuncture achieves its effects through the release of various peptides, most notably the opioids endorphin and dynorphin. In order to achieve this, it is thought to excite peripheral receptors or nerve fibers in much the same way as vigorous muscular exercise. Both exercise and acupuncture have been found to generate rhythmical discharges in the nerve fibers resulting in the central release of endogenous peptides. Although the areas of the brain where this release occurs

ABOVE Boxing causes direct damage to brain tissue and is hence widely condemned by doctors.

have not yet been identified, it is possible that it takes place within the periaqueductal gray, a region known to initiate inhibitions responsible for the reduction of pain. As to how acupuncture might provide therapy for mental disorders, there is preliminary evidence that it may interact with the central catecholamine systems that are implicated in some of these conditions.

Why do so many doctors and medical researchers disapprove of boxing?

The brain is encased within the bony box of the skull, and protected by fluid and sheets of strong tissue. Nevertheless, when battered by deliberately targeted blows, this protection is inadequate. Given the annual death toll in boxing, it is reasonable to assume that there are numerous cases of minor damage that pass unnoticed until the individual concerned has accumulated a critical number. This is not a field of human activity that lends itself to controlled study, since no two punches are identical, and currently brain scanning is unable to detect microscopic damage. Moreover, when it comes to assessing the damage that results from boxing, too many interested parties offer unconvincing reassurances, and a ringside doctor is hardly a substitute for a neurosurgery team.

Nevertheless, statistical studies carried out on the boxing population indicate significant risks, and there is even a form of dementia that owes its name to the sport – dementia pugilistica. Postmortem studies have shown that the principal dangers to the brain resulting from a punch are torsion inside the skull and ensuing hemorrhages. There are also tearing effects, sometimes resulting in rupture of the tissue that separates the main reservoirs of cerebrospinal fluid, the lateral ventricles.

So long as the head remains a legitimate target and rendering your opponent unconscious remains the most effective way of winning, boxing will be an abhorrent spectacle to anyone who values the organ of personality, intelligence, and humanity.

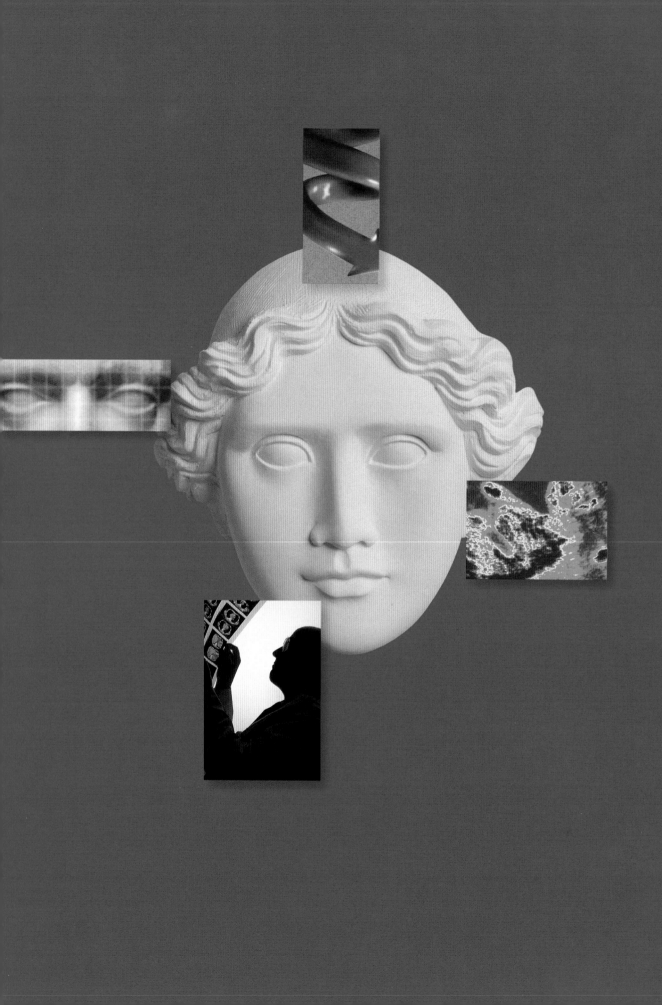

chapter seven

science and the brain

There are still many areas where the brain has yet to yield up its secrets, so what does the future hold for brain research?

Science and the Brain

We have now reached the end of our journey through the mysteries of the brain, a journey that begins in the womb and continues right up to our last moments. We have looked at the physiology and chemistry of the brain, its architectural structure, and its electrical communication system. We have explored the complex relationship between the brain we are born with and the brain that grows from our experiences. And we have investigated the enormous range of tasks that the brain performs on our behalf, and the sometimes devastating consequences that can result from any disruption to its orderly workings. An enormous amount of research is being carried out across the world with hundreds of thousands of dollars worth of equipment. So is it true to say that we are at a position in brain research where the secrets of the mind are at our fingertips?

The answer, as with so many aspects of our investigations of the brain, is yes and no. Immense strides have been made over the last 30 years in expanding our knowledge, particularly at the micro-level of cellular structure. In the mid-twentieth century treatment to address brain disorders was crude and haphazard, and any therapeutic benefit that occurred was more by luck than judgment. Our increased understanding of the brain at the chemical level has allowed the development of drug therapies that can bring about dramatic improvements in the lives of people suffering from conditions like Parkinson's disease, depression, and schizophrenia. However, as one of our contributors commented earlier, we have really only got to grips with a fraction of what there is to discover about the brain's capacities.

BELOW It is impossible, outside the realms of science fiction, to replace the brain with a microchip. The human brain is an organic structure, and no machine could replicate its dynamic, living qualities.

There are several reasons for caution when making any claims for the extent of our knowledge. One is that the brain is not an isolated entity, but rather part of a body system from which it receives constant feedback. This is one reason why the idea of the brain as a computer is so flawed; rather than being mechanical, the brain is an organic, living thing and its character and structure change from moment to moment. The dynamics of neuronal activity are such that cells are constantly competing with each other, reacting to inputs and sending impulses, and dying altogether. Any model of the brain has to take account of this constant restlessness.

The same criticism can be made of studies that claim to have isolated the gene for criminality or homosexuality. Moving simplistically from the cellular level to the level of behavior disregards the sheer complexity of neuronal activity and the influence of environmental factors in our development.

Perhaps the most important indicator of the limits of our knowledge is the issue of consciousness, the mind's "awareness" that it is doing what it is doing. This dimension of the brain's functioning is not one that admits of investigation at the level of cells, chemicals, and synapses, which is perhaps why some scientists reject the very notion of consciousness. Nonetheless, this is one of the central mysteries of the mind, and we have scarcely begun to comprehend it.

At the end of the Decade of the Brain we are aware as never before of how much remains to be discovered about the brain – but we have have also put in place the cornerstones on which to build our knowledge into the next millennium.

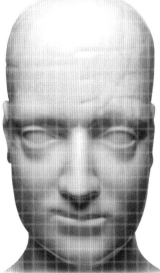

RIGHT Scientific appreciation of the brain and its complexities has moved a long way from the brain-mapping fixation of the phrenologists.

The brain and the future

Having looked at the human brain from the point of view of its evolution, its structure, and its function, it is now possible to make some suggestions as to what the future holds. The six contributors to this book here offer their views on how our knowledge of the brain will be put to use in this century.

PHARMACOLOGIST GREGORY BACON

SCIENCE HAS GIVEN US many confident answers to our questions about the universe. When it comes to the brain, however, we are still taking our first hesitant steps toward a complete understanding of its complexity. A lot of data has been accumulated, but it has yet to be unified into a complete understanding of the quintessence of the human brain. It may be that the sheer intricacy of the brain will defeat the attempts of the most highly trained minds, assisted by the most powerful computers, to unravel its secrets.

The neuropharmacological study of the brain has employed many techniques traditional to classical pharmacology, including the use of pharmacological tools and the investigation of chemical deficiencies apparent in disabled patients. The next great advances in the neurosciences will not necessarily involve the study of deficient brains, but may concentrate on intact, fully functioning systems. Modern imaging techniques have allowed scientists to perform quite advanced measurements of brain function without resorting to invasive, potentially disruptive equipment, and have opened up whole new fields of research.

Meanwhile we can make the most of our own brains, even though we still do not know exactly how they work. While no one would conceivably want, or even be able, to run his or her brain at full throttle all the time, there is certainly scope for improvement. Although neurons do not proliferate once mature, their dendrites and axons are still free to branch and make connections with other neurons. Since it is the number and intricacy of the connections – rather than the number of neurons – that is the key to the brain's complexity, any increase in the number of synapses is likely to produce an enhancement of brain function.

The plasticity of the brain is at its greatest when we are young, during the period most critical for development, but it can remain strong well into old age. However, if the brain is to continue to run efficiently, it is important to keep it well exercised, just like any other part of the body. With training, new tasks can be tackled and old skills improved. And one day it may even be possible to use pharmacology to aid the formation of new synapses, by administering neuronal growth factors. Life in the neurosciences promises to continue to be one of discovery and illumination.

ABOVE The brain: will we ever get to the bottom of it? We are continually acquiring more knowledge, yet still seem far from penetrating its complex workings.

ANATOMIST CLIVE COEN

IN ORDER TO ASSESS the prospects for improving our brains, we need to consider some of the basic constraints on this organ. There are only six natural routes into it: the five senses and ingestion. Furthermore, in broad terms, the brain has only two ways of affecting the world outside its immediate confines: by moving muscles and controlling hormones, actions that are often not only beyond our conscious control but beyond our consciousness. It's only through muscles and hormones that the brain can communicate with the outside world – by using, for example, speech muscles to make a telephone call, or antidiuretic hormone to control the kidneys.

Motor neuron disease is devastating, but it spares the neuroendocrine system and involuntary muscles such as the heart. Unfortunately, these offer no useful routes for communicating ideas and emotions to the outside world. Because the renowned physicist Stephen Hawking is severely afflicted by this disease, the only access we have to his mind is via the few voluntary muscles that he can still use to control his voice synthesizer. In the face of such fortitude, we might do well to ask ourselves whether we are putting our own muscles and hormones to optimal use.

There is no single site that could provide an interface between the brain's diverse components and the outside world. This may well mean that completely novel ways of transferring information between the brain and artificial devices (e.g. downloading specific memories to a silicon chip) will never be feasible. To be realistic, the current options for developing and maintaining an optimally functioning brain are still the ones that have always existed – to give it the best opportunities and to avoid damaging it in any way.

"You are what you eat" is a relevant maxim in this context. The most enduring effects of famine can be seen in the babies whose brains are permanently impaired by inadequate nutrition. Ingestion also covers the various ways in which we saturate our central nervous system with recreational drugs – alcohol being the most widespread. Such practices are at a cost that's not fully understood.

What about the other routes into the brain, apart from the dietary ones? Sensory deprivation has long been recognized as one of the most effective ways of breaking the human will. Recent brain-scanning studies of Romanian orphans neglected in infancy have confirmed the deleterious effects of environmental deprivation. It's increasingly clear that a varied and stimulating environment is important for all brains, not just those of the young and the elderly.

Finally, there is an obvious but by no means universally accepted piece of advice that is well worth heeding: if you want to look after your brain, avoid blows to the head. The advantages of wearing a helmet are now recognized by motorcyclists and bicyclists, but still largely ignored by skiers, soccer players and, of course, boxers. Current research suggests that one of the best ways to increase your chances of getting Alzheimer's disease is to sustain a severe blow to the head in late middle age.

In summary, to improve human brainpower, support continued research on this delicate and magnificent organ, and take great care of your own. Either use it or lose it.

BELOW We know how important it is to protect our brains. Our sturdy cranium gives us a head start (so to speak), but further precautions are in order.

CLINICAL NEUROSCIENTIST AND SURGEON HENRY MARSH

WE LIVE IN AN AGE of scientific materialism where it is assumed that everything, including our thoughts and feelings, can be reduced to simple physical causes and effects. Although modern physics, with the uncertainty of quantum mechanics, views things slightly differently, the words written by the poet Matthew Arnold more than 150 years ago seem to summarize the scientific dogma of our age:

> …the world, which seems
> To lie before us like a land of dreams,
> So various, so beautiful, so new,
> Hath really neither joy, nor love, nor light,
> Nor certitude, nor peace, nor help for pain…

Our feelings, our loves, our opinions are frequently depicted as being no more than chemicals or the product of our genes. However, I would argue that a proper understanding of the brain shows this view to be profoundly mistaken.

Thinking is hard work. One quarter of the blood pumped by the heart each minute goes to the brain. Modern brain scans show that when we are thinking, blood flow to the relevant part of the brain increases. There is plenty of evidence to show that young animals placed in a stimulating and interesting environment develop more complex connections between their brain cells than similar animals deprived of such experience. Also, that the risk of Alzheimer's disease is greater in people who leave school early in adolescence. We improve our brains by thinking, and I worry that the success of scientific materialism in giving us a convenient and comfortable existence will produce in our children the intellectual equivalent of the obesity that is increasingly prevalent in modern society. I am not suggesting that everyone should undergo the intellectual equivalent of circuit training; but just as athletes become fit by discipline and training, so we have to exert our minds if we wish to improve our brains.

It is entirely possible that at some point in the future our brains will eventually be reduced by scientific explanation to something akin to the operating system of a digital computer. However, what cannot be reduced in this way, and what is more important to us as personalities than anything else, is our individual consciousness. I experience a sense of utter awe and astonishment when I reflect that the same materials (hydrogen, carbon, nitrogen, and other elements) that make up the tree that I can see in my backyard are also the components of the conscious self that is thinking and writing these words. It is a quite wonderful thought — a thought that is itself composed of hydrogen, carbon, nitrogen, and other elements.

ABOVE The confluence of natural elements in the world around us creates what we perceive as wonderful. Our brains, similarly, are an extraordinary result of something that has evolved naturally.

LEFT Is there a danger that the marvels of technology that delivers everything we need to the comfort of our homes are having a damaging effect on our capacity to think and imagine?

DEVELOPMENTAL PSYCHOLOGIST KIM PLUNKETT

ACCORDING TO THE classic textbooks on developmental neuro-biology, we are born with just about all the neurons we'll ever have, and by 12 months of age the overwhelming majority of connections (synapses) between those neurons have been established. Thereafter, the development of the central nervous system consists of two processes: the fine tuning of existing connections and cell death (we lose millions of neurons every day). This might seem like a pretty bleak outlook for improvement – but throughout most of our adult life we are able to learn new facts about the world, acquire new skills, and even to learn new languages (albeit imperfectly), so evidently there's a lot that can be achieved through fine tuning of existing connections. In addition, recent research has questioned the assumption that the creation of new neurons and the growth of new connections cease shortly after birth. Under the right conditions, it is possible that new growth can and does occur well into adulthood.

We still need to understand in greater depth just how the brain changes in response to experience. We know that human knowledge, both practical and theoretical, is represented by the pattern of connections between neurons in the brain – and that learning new facts and skills involves changing that pattern of connectivity. One of the most fruitful ways to improve our understanding of this process is to study learning in children. We still know relatively little about the way in which brain development influences the development of mental abilities in children, but researchers have invented ingenious techniques for investigating the basic abilities of infants and young children. Consequently, we now have a much more precise picture of what they can do instinctively and what they have to learn.

Moreover, new methods have become available for studying the way brain activity changes during development. These methods have yet to be fully exploited, but there is now a real chance of discovering how brain development and mental development are linked. Perhaps once we have established a better understanding of how this process occurs naturally in young children, we will then be better placed to suggest therapeutic methods for people with brain damage or to enhance the abilities that normally functioning individuals already possess.

Since we are now building ever more sophisticated computer models of the brain using artificial neural networks, it is not a science-fiction fantasy to suppose that a time will soon arrive when it is possible to introduce silicon-based transplants into carbon-based brains to facilitate or enhance functioning. We already utilize cochlea transplants, when necessary, for people whose hearing is impaired. The use of artificial neural networks for more central cortical processing is an obvious extension of this trend. Does this mean that our personalities and unique identity will be lost? Almost certainly not. The uniqueness of any individual stems from the enormous complexity of the human brain, and it is unlikely that even highly complicated artificial systems will match the complexity of the most complicated machine known to us – the human brain – even by the end of the twenty-first century.

ABOVE Children have all the essential mental ingredients at an early age. What happens as they grow is mainly memory-building and fine tuning of connections.

PSYCHOLOGIST, SPECIALIZING IN LEARNING AND MEMORY **NICHOLAS RAWLINS**

THE BRAIN, when working at its best, does an amazing job. It manages to fit a fantastic amount of computing power into a small and readily portable package. However, it's important to remember that the brain isn't a machine with a blueprint that specifies exactly the way it is to be built: the "finished product" is a result both of initial design and of experience during development. So the way our brain ends up is partly determined by our environments. To an extent we, and those who care for us in infancy, have control over that. Once development is over, it's not long before the process of aging starts pruning our brain cells; and the rate at which that happens may also partly be under our influence.

We can care for our own brains, and our children's brains, in several ways. Let's start with development. Almost from the moment they are born, infants interact with the people around them; their brains are preprogrammed to do that. Those interactions all help to select particular connections to be strengthened. And as that happens, other potential connections quietly wither away. The evidence suggests that the richer the environment is, the more complex the eventual structures of the brain cells will be, and that we can therefore help to maximize their potential. The evidence also suggests that the key to keeping the brain healthy is to keep it active and stimulated throughout life.

So far, modern medicine has been able to do little about our aging brains, though it keeps our bodies going for longer and longer. Greater and greater proportions of the population now suffer from age-related degeneration of the brain. Is there anything that can be done to help? We may well develop treatments that slow down or prevent degeneration. But there seem to be even more radical possibilities on the horizon. There has already been a tiny handful of successful neural transplant operations, in which new brain cells have been injected into the brain to replace dead cells. Some of the new cells survive and form connections that go some way to restoring normal function.

At present, these techniques have only very limited applications, but the technology is advancing rapidly. Recent work on animals has shown that developing cells can be introduced into the brain and will connect up to the existing cells. Amazingly, these "stem cells" have the potential to become any of the many different kinds of brain cells; they migrate through the brain and tend to turn into whatever kinds of cells are missing. Neural transplants of this kind may offer ways to rebuild our brains. Would we still be ourselves after such treatment? My own view is that in essence we would be, since the new cells would be hugely outnumbered by our existing brain cells with their well-established circuitry and connections. If the new cells simply integrated with these and patched in some missing pieces, then it's conceivable that they might enable our own damaged circuits to work properly again. And with luck, that would return us to our former selves. It's quite possible that we may start to see the answers within the next few years.

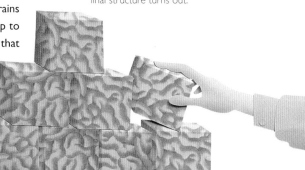

BELOW The building blocks of the brain are given to us at conception, but we can exert a lot of influence over the way the final structure turns out.

PHYSIOLOGIST JOHN STEIN

THE MAIN SCOURGES of modern humanity come at the beginning and end of life, impairing the development of the brain during childhood and causing its degeneration in old age. Poverty and hardship frequently result in poor nutrition of the brain in unborn babies and infants, and can also cause emotional and cultural deprivation. These factors, if coupled with an unfavorable genetic heritage, limit the flowering of a child's intelligence and impose depressing limits on his or her future. All too often this leads to frustration, loss of hope, and despair, followed by a descent into drug addiction, vandalism, and crime. Clearly, a downward spiral of this kind can have a variety of ingredients, genetic, economic, and social. Many would argue that the most important of these is economic, and that eradicating poverty would solve the problem. But deprivation will probably be with us forever, no matter how affluent the world becomes.

A more promising course of action might be to take steps to improve the physical and psychological environment of the developing brains of children, so that they are better equipped to compensate for deprivation. Research makes it increasingly clear that particular nutrients, such as essential fatty acids, are important at certain stages of brain development. Supplements of these, given at the right time as part of a child-health program, would probably do more to alleviate unhappiness and crime than a ten percent hike in national income.

ABOVE We can do little to address a child's genetic inheritance, but its mental development can be nurtured through the provision of a positive environment.

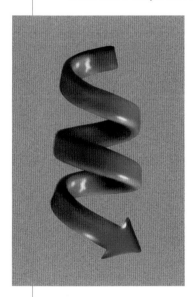

It also seems probable that, because of the youthful brain's plasticity, properly timed and targeted training could enable it to compensate for a variety of impairments. This has already been shown to be beneficial in the field of dyslexia. Given greater understanding of their causes, it is conceivable that conditions such as cerebral palsy, epilepsy, autism, depression, and even schizophrenia might respond to similar treatment.

The various forms of brain degeneration encountered toward the end of life are among the most distressing of all ailments. However, here, too, there is hope for the future, because eventually, as we come to understand the pathology of these conditions in greater detail, we should be able to diagnose them at an earlier stage. There will then be a possibility of halting the degenerative processes before serious damage occurs. In the meantime, it is likely that we will be able to develop ways of helping the brain overcome the effects of degeneration. Precision surgery to the basal ganglia to alleviate the motor disorders of Parkinson's disease could be a first step in this direction. And soon it should be possible to time and target stimulation of structures to take over the function of damaged regions, or even to replace them by implanting undamaged neurons grown for the purpose.

LEFT New methods are being developed all the time to address the downward spiral of brain degeneration as a result of illness or old age.

reference

Glossary

Further reading

Contributors

Index

Glossary

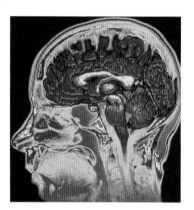

5-HT

see serotonin

ACETYLCHOLINE

A neurotransmitter, also known as ACh. Acetylcholine is active at all nerve–muscle junctions and many other places in the nervous systems. Any action involving acetylcholine is called a cholinergic reaction, and may be blocked by anticholinergic drugs.

ADRENALIN

A hormone, also known as epinephrine. It is one of the two hormones, with noradrenalin, secreted by the adrenal glands in response to stress – producing in the body the classic "fight or flight" reaction, including raised heart rate, opening of the airways, and narrowing of the blood vessels.

AMINES

A huge group of naturally occurring organic chemicals. In the body, amines make up an important group of neurotransmitters called the catecholamines which include dopamine, noradrenalin, and adrenalin.

AMINO ACID

The basic chemicals of life. All proteins are made from 20 different amino acids. The body can make 10 of these. The remaining ten (eight in adults), called essential acids, must be taken in in the diet.

AMYGDALA

A structure that it is part of the limbic system in the middle of the brain. It is where we remember things that frightened us.

ANTAGONIST

An agonist is a neurotransmitter, drug, or other molecule that stimulates receptors in nerve gaps to produce a certain reaction. An antagonist is a drug or other molecule that blocks the receptors that take up agonists.

APHASIA

Strictly speaking, a complete loss of language skills. The term is more usually used interchangeably with dysphasia to describe a disturbance in a person's ability to understand words or speak, often as a result of a stroke.

AXON

The long tail of a nerve cell by which the cell sends signals to target cells. Hundreds of thousands of axons bundled together make up a nerve.

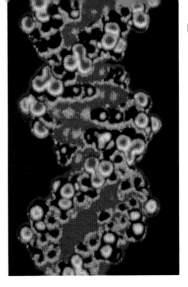

BASAL GANGLIA

A bundle of nerves in the middle of the brain, including the caudate nucleus and substantia nigra. It links your commands to move from the cortex with the coordination skills of the cerebellum.

BLINDSIGHT

A form of blindness in which the eyes and nerves are perfectly healthy, but there is damage to the visual cortex where the brain registers what we see. A person with blindsight could point reliably at lights, but would not be aware he or she was seeing them.

BRAINSTEM

The "root" of the brain at the top of the spinal cord. All signals between the body and the brain pass through the brainstem.

CATECHOLAMINE

see amine

CEREBELLUM

The pool-ball-sized lump at the back of the brain that controls balance and coordination.

CEREBRAL CORTEX

The wrinkly outside of the brain where sensations such as sight and touch are registered and all our conscious thoughts take place.

CHOLINERGIC

see acetylcholine

CORPUS CALLOSUM

The bridge of nerves between the two halves of the brain.

CORTICOSTEROIDS

Corticosteroid hormones are made in the adrenal glands control the way the body uses nutrients and excretes salt and water in the urine. Corticosteroid drugs work in the same way as the corticosteroid hormones and are used to treat a huge range of illnesses.

DEMENTIA

A general decline in mental ability often associated with aging. It is usually caused by brain disease and is progressive, making victims vague and forgetful.

DENDRITES

One of the many branching connecting threads of a nerve cell.

DEPRESSANT

A drug such alcohol or barbiturates which depresses or slows down the activity of the nervous system. Small doses raise the mood; high doses make people moody, anxious, and irritable, as well as slowing reflexes, slurring speech, and upsetting balance.

DNA OR DEOXYRIBO-NUCLEIC ACID

DNA is the complex double-spiral shaped molecule inside every single living cell that carries all the cell's instructions for life, and the complete genetic information to make a new organism, whether it is a bacterium or a human being.

DOPAMINE

A neurotransmitter found in the brain and around some blood vessels. It plays an important part in the control of body movements and a lack of dopamine in the basal ganglia is linked to Parkinson's disease.

EEG

Electroencephalogram, a device which records the electrical activity of the brain. The electricity from individual nerve impulses is too small to pick up but an EEG picks up the combined effect of many impulses to show things such as the pattern of brain waves during sleep.

ENDOCRINE SYSTEM

The system of hormones carried around in the bloodstream to control the activity of various organs around the body.

ENDORPHINS

The body's own painkiller susbtances – neurotransmitters made in the brain that create cellular and behavioral effects similar to those of morphine.

ENKEPHALINS

Small protein molecules made in the brain and nerve endings that act as natural painkillers and heighten mood.

EPILEPSY

A tendency to have repeated seizures or a temporary change in the way the brain works that can result from a huge a variety of causes including birth trauma, brain tumors, and strokes.

FORAMEN MAGNUM

The large hole in the base of the skull through which the spinal cord passes out to the rest of the body.

GABA

Gamma-amino butyric acid, an amino acid transmitter in the brain whose main function is to inhibit the firing of neurons.

GENES

The body's chemical instructions for life – for growing up, surviving, having children, and perhaps even for dying. Individual genes are instructions to make a particular protein. Groups of genes are instructions to make a particular feature, such as the color of hair, or create a process such as digesting fat.

GLIA, GLIAL CELLS

Specialized cells that nourish and support neurons.

GRAY MATTER

Regions of the brain and spinal cord made mainly of densely packed nuclei of nerve cells (see white matter).

HIPPOCAMPUS

A seahorse-shaped structure in the limbic system involved in memories, learning, and emotion.

HISTAMINE

A chemical released during an allergic reaction by cells – especially cells in body tissues called mast cells. It causes the redness and swelling of inflammation. Its effects are reduced by antihistamine drugs.

HOMEOSTASIS

The dynamic process by which an organism maintains its internal environment in complete balance no matter what happens outside.

HORMONE

Chemicals released by endocrine and other glands to control the activity of certain target cells and playing a major role in such things as growth, fear reactions, and sexual changes.

HYPOTHALAMUS

A tiny, complex bundle of nerves about the size of a cherry in the middle of the brain that regulates the body's automatic internal nervous system and controls things such as blood pressure, heart rate, hunger, thirst, and sexual desire.

LIMBIC SYSTEM

A large Y-shaped formation of nerves, including the amygdala, hippocampus, septum, and basal ganglia, wrapped around the brainstem and linking the lower parts of the brain with the cerebrum. It is involved in emotions, memory, smell, and certain aspects of movement.

LOBE

The lobes of the cerebrum are its four rounded-end quarters: the frontal, parietal, temporal, and occipital.

MDMA

Methylenedioxymethamphetamine is the hallucinogenic drug better known as ecstasy or E. It has a huge a range of effects including an extreme mood and energy boost, restlessness, raised body temperature, and nausea.

MEDULLA OR MEDULLA OBLONGATA

The lowest part of the brainstem below the pons and above the spinal cord.

NARCOTIC

Strong painkilling drugs including opium-related drugs such as heroin, morphine, and codeine. Drug abusers take them for the relaxed euphoria or "high" they give.

NEURON

A nerve cell. It transmits signals carrying information via a long fiber called the axon, and collects impulses via shorter branches called dendrites.

NEURONAL PATHWAYS

The routes that nerve signals take through the spinal cord, divided into ascending pathways taking sensory signals to the brain and descending pathways taking motor (muscle-movement) signals from the brain to the body.

NEUROTRANSMITTER

A chemical released by a nerve cell at a synapse to pass on a nerve signal via receptors on another nerve cell.

NORADRENALIN

A chemical neurotransmitter and hormone released both in the brain and by the adrenal glands. It seems to be involved in arousal, reward, and regulation of sleep and mood, and the regulation of blood pressure.

PARASYMPATHETIC NERVOUS SYSTEM

see sympathetic nervous system

PEPTIDES

Chains of amino acids that can function as neurotransmitters or hormones.

PINEAL GLAND

A tiny bundle of nerves right in the very center of the brain, sometimes called the third eye because it responds to changing light levels from the eyes to set the body's clock.

PITUITARY GLAND

A gland in the middle of the brain closely linked to the hypothalamus that secretes many important hormones

PONS

A bundle of 30,000 nerves linking the spinal cord and the cerebellum and controlling heart rhythms, breathing, and sleep and dreams.

PROTEINS

The large organic molecules from which all living things are built, including fibrous proteins which are insoluble and form the structure of many body tissues, and globular proteins which are soluble and make up body chemicals such as hormones.

PSYCHOSIS

A condition of being so psychologically disturbed as to lose touch with the real world.

RECEPTOR

Specialized sensory cells designed to pick up and transmit sensory information.

RETICULAR FORMATION, THE

A tight bundle of nerves in the brainstem that acts as the brain's filter system.

SEROTONIN

A neurotransmitter (also called 5-HT) in the brain and in the gut thought to play many roles including sending you to sleep and temperature regulation. Some antidepressant drugs are targeted to serotonin systems.

STIMULANTS

Substances such as caffeine, nicotine, amphetamine (speed), cocaine, and MDMA (ecstasy) that in small doses wake you up by exciting the central nervous system, and in high doses make you anxious and even psychotic.

SUBSTANTIA NIGRA

Literally "black substance," a nucleus of cells in the brainstem that is the source of the neurotransmitter dopamine.

SYMPATHETIC NERVOUS SYSTEM & PARASYMPATHETIC NERVOUS SYSTEM

The sympathetic nervous system and parasympathetic nervous system are the two opposing parts of the body's autonomic nervous system – the automatic internal system that controls body functions such as digestion.

SYNAPSE

The tiny gap between two nerve endings across which nerve signals are transmitted by chemicals called neurotransmitters.

THALAMUS

Two walnut-sized masses of nerve tissue in the middle of the brain which relay and filter sensory information flowing into the brain.

TREPANNING

The ancient practice of drilling holes in the skull, supposedly to relieve pressure on the brain.

VASOPRESSIN

An alternative name for ADH or antidiuretic hormone which reduces the flow of water from the body as urine.

VENTRICLES

Four large spaces filled with cerebrospinal fluid – three in the brain and one in the brainstem.

WHITE MATTER

Regions of the brain and spinal cord consisting mainly of the long axons (tails) of nerve cells (*see gray matter*).

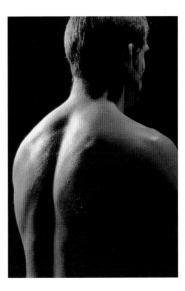

Further reading

BLUM, DEBORAH,
Sex on the Brain
(Viking Penguin, 1998)

BODEN, MARGARET,
The Creative Mind (Abacus, 1990)

CALVIN, WILLIAM H.,
How Brains Think
(Weidenfeld & Nicolson, 1997)

COLLINS, HARRY,
*Artificial Experts: Social Knowledge
and Intelligent Machines*
(Cambridge University Press, 1990)

CRICK, FRANCIS,
The Astonishing Hypothesis
(Touchstone Books, 1995)

CSIKSZENTMIHALYI, MIHALY,
Living Well (Weidenfeld &
Nicolson, 1997)

DAMASIO, ANTONIO R.,
*Descartes' Error: Emotion,
Reason and the Human Brain*
(Picador, 1995)

DEACON, TERENCE,
*The Symbolic Species: The
Co-Evolution of Language and
the Human Brain* (Allen Lane,
1997)

DENNETT, DANIEL,
Consciousness Explained
(Allen Lane, 1992)

DONALDSON, MARGARET,
Children's Minds (Penguin, 1979)

DONALDSON, MARGARET,
Human Minds: An Exploration
(Penguin, 1992)

DUBOVSKY, STEVEN L.,
Mind-Body Deceptions
(W. W. Norton, 1997)

EDELMAN, GERALD,
Bright Air, Brilliant Fire
(Allen Lane, 1992)

GARDNER, HOWARD,
Extraordinary Minds
(Weidenfeld & Nicolson, 1997)

GAZZANIGA, MICHAEL S.,
*Nature's Mind: The Biological
Roots of Thinking, Emotions,
Sexuality, Language and
Intelligence* (Penguin, 1992)

GOLEMAN, DANIEL,
*Emotional Intelligence: Why
It Can Matter More than* IQ
(Bloomsbury, 1996)

GREENFIELD, SUSAN,
The Human Brain: A Guided Tour
(Weidenfeld & Nicolson, 1997)

GREENFIELD, SUSAN (ED.),
*The Human Mind Explained:
The Control Centre of the Living
Machine* (Cassell, 1996)

HOBSON, J. ALAN,
*The Chemistry of Conscious States:
How the Brain Changes Its Mind*
(Little, Brown, 1994)

KOHN, MAREK,
*As We Know It: Coming to Terms
with the Evolved Mind* (Granta,
1999)

LEDOUX, JOSEPH,
The Emotional Brain
(Simon & Schuster, 1998)

LURIA, A.A.,
The Mind of a Mnemonist
(Jonathan Cape, 1969)

MARTIN, PAUL,
The Sickening Mind
(Harper Collins, 1997)

MITHEN, STEVEN,
*The Prehistory of the Mind:
A Search for the Origins of Art,
Religion and Science*
(Thames & Hudson, 1996)

ORNSTEIN, ROBERT,
*The Right Mind: Making Sense of
the Hemispheres* (Roundhouse,
1997)

PENROSE, ROGER,
Shadows of the Mind
(Oxford University Press, 1994)

PERT, CANDACE,
Molecules of Emotion
(Simon & Schuster, 1997)

PINKER, STEVEN,
How the Mind Works (Allen Lane,
1997)

ROSE, STEPHEN,
Lifelines (Allen Lane, 1997)

ROSE, STEPHEN,
*The Making of Memory:
From Molecules to Mind*
(Bantam Press, 1993)

SACKS, OLIVER,
An Anthropologist on Mars
(Picador, 1995)

SACKS, OLIVER,
Awakenings (Picador, 1982)

SACKS, OLIVER,
*The Man Who Mistook His Wife
for a Hat* (Summit Books, 1985)

WINNER, ELLEN,
*Gifted Children: Myths and
Realities* (Basic Books, 1996)

ZEKI, SEMIR,
A Vision of the Brain
(Blackwell Scientific, 1993)

Contributors

SUSAN GREENFIELD

Susan Greenfield is Professor of Pharmacology at Oxford University and lectures all over the world on consciousness and the mind. Her many books include *The Human Brain: A Guided Tour* and the best-selling *Journey to the Centre of the Mind.*

GREGORY BACON

Gregory Bacon studied neuroscience as an undergraduate, where he developed an interest in neuropharmacology. He has subsequently embarked upon post-graduate research at Oxford University, studying the neuroanatomical interactions of central serotonergic and dopaminergic systems.

CLIVE COEN

Clive Coen is Professor of Neuroscience at King's College, London. His research interests focus on the brain's control of biological rhythms and reproductive hormones.

HENRY MARSH

Henry Marsh is Senior Consultant Neurosurgeon at Atkinson Morley's Hospital in London. His clinical specialism is the surgical removal of brain tumors, and he has also worked extensively to introduce modern neurosurgical methods with colleagues in the Ukraine.

NICHOLAS RAWLINS

Nicholas Rawlins is Professor of Behavioral Neuroscience at Oxford University and Tutor in Psychology at University College Oxford. He has published more than 100 scholarly articles on the workings of the brain.

KIM PLUNKETT

Kim Plunkett is Professor of Cognitive Neuroscience at Oxford University, with a special interest in linguistic and cognitive development in young children. Among his many books are *Rethinking Innateness* (MIT Press, 1996) and *Language Acquisition and Connectionist Psychology* (Psychology Press, 1998).

JOHN STEIN

Professor John Stein lectures in physiology at Oxford University Medical School and is Tutorial Fellow in Medicine at Magdalen College, Oxford University. He is particularly interested in eye and limb movement disorders in neurological patients and in developmental dyslexics.

Index

Acknowledgments

The publishers are grateful to the following for permission to reproduce copyright material

ARCHIV FUR KUNST UND GESCHICHTE
pps. 10T, 98, 106BR, 124R

ERIC LESSING/AKG
pps. 9T(Louvre), 150(PRADO)

CORBIS
pps. 121, 141B.

THE IMAGE BANK
pps. 37, 51TL, 68T, 83TR, 88B, 99T,
109MBR+BR, 111TR, 131T, 169.

IMAGES COLOUR LIBRARY
p. 160.

REX FEATURES
pps. 85, 95B.

THE SCIENCE PHOTO LIBRARY
pps. 13B, 13R, 20R, 30B, 32B, 33B,
41T, 91, 117BL, 118T.

THE STOCKMARKET
pps. 8TR, 9R, 10B,11, 16T, 20BL, 77TL,
78TL, 90TR, 118B, 127, 130L, 131B, 136L, 152, 166.

SUPERSTOCK
pps. 15T, 50TL, 59BR, 61TL, 89L, 89R,
105T (Diana Ong) 109BL+ TR + MTR, 125B, 132T.

TONY STONE IMAGES
pps. 8BL, 15R, 21, 24T, 25BL, 25TR, 26MR, 26BR,
28, 40BL, 40TR, 46TL, 48T, 57BR, 69BR, 72T, 74TR,
75BL, 78BR, 86T, 90/91, 105BR, 110T, 115B, 126,
137T, 137B, 140T, 176.